GOOD OLD DAYS PRESENTS
HOMETOWN
MEMORIES

Edited by Ken and Janice Tate

HOUSE of
WHITE
BIRCHES

PUBLISHERS
SINCE 1947

Editors: Ken and Janice Tate
Associate Editor: Barb Sprunger
Copy Editors: Läna Schurb, Cathy Reef

Production Coordinator: Brenda Gallmeyer
Creative Coordinator: Shaun Venish
Design/Production Artist: Beverly Jenkins
Traffic Coordinator: Sandra Beres
Production Assistants: Carol Dailey, Chad Tate

Photography: Tammy Christian
Photography Assistant: Linda Quinlan
Photography Stylist: Arlou Wittwer

Publishers: Carl H. Muselman, Arthur K. Muselman
Chief Executive Officer: John Robinson
Marketing Director: Scott Moss
Editorial Director: Vivian Rothe
Production Director: George Hague

Printed in the United States of America
First Printing: 1999
Library of Congress Number: 99-94092
ISBN: 1-882138-43-0

We would like to thank the following for the photos and art prints used in this book:
Apple Creek Publishing: "Summer Breeze" by Doug Knutson, page 135; "The Washroom"
by Doug Knutson, page 136. Both by arrangement with Apple Creek Publishing,
Cedar Rapids, IA 52402, (800) 662-1707.
Mill Pond Press: "The Immigrant Spirit" by Jim Daly, page 38; "Melodies Remembered" by Greg Olsen,
page 93; "Territorial Rights" by Jim Daly, page 112. All by arrangement with Mill Pond Press Inc.
For information on art prints, contact Mill Pond Press, Venice, FL 34292, (800) 535-0331.
Wild Wings Inc.: "Saturday Afternoon at the Movies" by Lee Dubin, page 33; "Turn of the Century
Drugstore" by Lee Dubin, page 44, 129; "Silent Night" by Sam Timm, page 141. All by arrangement
with Wild Wings Inc., Lake City, MN 55041, (800) 445-4833.
First Bank of Berne: Photos courtesy of First Bank of Berne, Berne, Ind., pages 25, 26.

Dear Friends of the Good Old Days,

When I was a youngster, growing up in the Ozark Mountains of southwest Missouri, school reunions were not the only ones held from year to year. Hometowns held them, too.

Whether they were called Old Home Days, or Town Reunion or some other moniker, present and former neighbors gathered each year to renew old friendships and strengthen the bonds that make Hometowns the backbone of any strong nation. Many families held their own reunions in conjunction with the town reunion. The whole festival seemed like Thanksgiving, Memorial Day and the Fourth of July all rolled into one to me.

There was always a feeling of bittersweet in those reunions. Folks became mistily nostalgic when they walked the streets of their youth, remembering what they left behind. Yes, most left for the big city for more opportunities and better jobs (or *any* job in some instances). But it's hard to remember that when you embrace a friend you haven't seen since childhood.

Perhaps it was that wonderful, ecstatic, poignant pain that led to the phrase, "You can't go home again."

In the 10 years that my wife, Janice, and I have produced *Good Old Days* magazine, we have seen that you *can* go home again. You can nod to neighbors on the street and stop at those same shops again. You can watch a parade, share "dinner on the grounds" at your old church and hear Mama calling you at twilight to come inside for supper.

This book is a reunion of sorts, reminding us of a time when a Hometown was not just where we were coming from, with dreams of going to. It was, more often than not, where Mama and Daddy grew up, met and married. It was where we were born, went to school, courted and wed our childhood beaus or sweethearts. It was where our souls remained—even if our bodies could not.

No, we *can* go home again. If fact, sometimes I think we must, if just to remind us where our roots are, where we came from. The Old Home Days between the covers of this book will take you with us back to those days again. This reunion will bring you smiles, laughter and, yes, some tears. But with every page you will be reminded of what made each and every Hometown so special.

Ken Tate

❧ Contents ❧

✦ Contents ✦

Uptown, Downtown

Chapter One

When the story of Americana is told, no chapter is greater or of more importance than that of Main Street, the downtown of every hometown in this great country. Downtown was where the "action" was—however little that might be in small towns and villages. Downtown was where the hubbub of commerce met the relaxed pleasure of friends and neighbors passing the time of day on a busy sidewalk.

Being a farm boy, my best memories of downtown are those of Saturdays back in the Good Old Days. We had a mid-'30s Chevy coupe, and almost every Saturday morning Mama, Grandma, Uncle Bob, my brother, sister and I crowded into that one-seater for what was then a long 10-mile trip to town. (We had three adults and my big brother squeezed across the bench seat, with baby sister in alternating laps. I stretched across the small platform, which filled the space from the top of the seat to the tiny back window of the coupe.)

The hustle and bustle of downtown was raucous music to the ears of a country boy used mainly to the bawling of cattle or the whirring song of the cicada during the summer. Grandma and Mama always wanted to make it to the mid-morning auction down by the feed store, where the auctioneer's chant and the bidders' shouts hypnotized me. After the auction we walked uptown, where the din of shoppers making their way from shop to shop was only surpassed by the rattle, roar and raucous horns of jalopies skirmishing at the intersections.

We walked Main Street to the "five and dime" store (and a nickel or a dime could actually buy something), or down Commercial Street to the Mercantile where Mama always liked to shop. Sometimes Mama left my brother and me with the old-timers seated at benches near the barbershop. There I learned the manly arts of whittling, spinning yarns and chewing tobacco. Whittling and yarn spinning have remained with me through all these years, but tobacco chewing lasted only until I mistakenly swallowed my cud. That was the shortest, most productive anti-tobacco campaign ever devised.

It was well past noon (my stomach told me more like 1:30 p.m.) when Mama and Grandma emerged from their shopping forays. Lunch was the Blue Plate special at the only diner in town, where I also sampled my first soft drink (at least the first one I can remember).

If the egg money went far enough, we kids were treated to the matinee at the Owens Theatre, with a western serial, newsreels (yuck!), cartoons (yea!) and a main feature. Shangri-La and popcorn, too—all for a quarter.

Downtown was glitz and glamour and lights after dark. From the pool hall and bar on the wrong side of the tracks to the drugstore with its ubiquitous soda fountain, downtown was everything this country boy could imagine.

As you read these memories, walk Uptown, Downtown with me and remember what it was like to stroll those sidewalks and look into those store windows with the wide-eyed amazement of youth. I can hear Mama calling, and there's always room for one more in the old Chevy coupe. Hometown memories are waiting—see you on Main Street!

—By Ken Tate

The Old Town Square

By Don Todd

Just the other day I passed through a friendly country village that sat clustered all around a sleepy, lazy square, and I couldn't help but nostalgically reflect on a square I used to know when we were both a trifle younger. A huge, round, polished, cherry-marble fountain stood gently brimming over in the center of my square and served as a momentary stopping place for all the busy crosstown, horse-drawn traffic.

Glistening, muscular cart horses paused beneath the bulging, lofty chestnut that swayed and rustled overhead, and sipped the fountain's sparkling waters in the chestnut's welcome spreading shade.

The fountain served as well as an alluring, playful splashing place for us baggy-shirted youngsters in floppy caps, scruffy boots, and pants with puffy knees.

Foot patrolmen with rows of shiny buttons on their stiffened tunics tipped their caps at passing ladies.

We, too, drank from its spilling waters and used it as a last excuse to tarry on the way to school. Then we greeted it exuberantly as a long-awaited friend, on the way back home.

Vehicular traffic crisscrossed through the square with sputters, roars and clatters.

Model-A's shimmied across, along with blunt-nosed trucks that growled with chain-drive gears. And now and then, a double-ended, boxy type of car, all black and silent, drifted by, sort of spiritlike, and made us kids just a little bit afraid.

Foot patrolmen with rows of shiny buttons on their stiffened tunics tipped their caps at passing ladies as the lawmen strolled their beats. As they strolled, they deftly twirled their awesome wooden "billies" as little knots of mischief-laden boys straggled past, their freckled poker faces full of well-disguised intentions.

Ladies dressed in shiny boots and somber, discreetly cut purple dresses swept back and forth across the square. Some wore black, snug-fitting hats, while others held their long-gloved hands to wide-brimmed straws that bent and twisted in the breeze. Still others trudged across with bulging, glossy canvas shopping bags, full of what would soon be conjured up as someone's tasty supper.

Groups of open-vested men stood knotted by the grocer's sidewalk bins, listening to the crackling, scratchy voice on radio describe a World

Then, slowly as the night drew down, the honk and haste of traffic died away and just the gentle hush of trees and hum of insects washed across the air.

Just beside the square, a bandstand stood upon the willowed common, where on Sunday afternoons and Wednesday evenings, the band in navy blue and red would strike up John Phillip Sousa marches, or float gently through sweet, nostalgic airs of *You Wonderful One* and *Ramona*.

While the older folks sat with rapt attention recalling memories of old, young lovers kissed and cuddled, and were occasionally befuddled by exasperating antics from some lurking youngsters, usually someone's younger brother.

Series game between Washington and New York. The aproned grocers rested jauntily up against their door jambs, twitched their brush mustaches and pushed back their summer "skimmers" as they joined in, listening to the Senators' Carl Hubbell pitch a shutout against the Giants.

Inside the open windows of the *Daily News*, typesetters and journalists in green eyeshades and rolled-up, pin-stripe sleeves set type and worried over bylines amid the hum and clack of rolling stock.

The shout of "Copyboy!" carried through smudged and screenless windows upon which a spread Blue Eagle had been pasted and was slowly wearing off.

And then a steam train, rushing somewhere through the growing dusk, would hoot and lilt a distant haunting note across the common and the square—then hoot again as it crowded Parson's Crossing, just to let you know it knew that it was there.

If you listened closely, you could hear the subtle, rhythmic clacking of the tracks; just as quickly it faded all away, as the rushing train passed down its predetermined course.

Then, as if to say it loathed leaving us, it strained across the ever-widening void of gloom and managed one more long and trailing note, as it hurried on its journey out across the lonesome black of night. ❖

The Town Pump

By Blanche Passa

The importance of the town pump should never be underestimated. Not only did it provide drinking water for most of the town folks, but for many farmers as well. The pump was mounted on a 3-foot square concrete slab some 20 feet from Daddy's lumberyard.

It wasn't really the *town* pump—it was Daddy's. He drilled the well, set it up and maintained it. But everyone knew they were welcome to use it because—well, that's just the way small towns are.

Every year Daddy sent a sample of water away to the state health department to have it tested to make sure it was safe for drinking. The water was cold and pure. Why, there were only two or three times that I can remember someone pumping up a dead mouse. Then Mama sent us kids over to pump the well dry. Then we had to pour a gallon of bleach down, wait a spell and pump the well dry again. Soon the well filled again with clean water. The water was good. Everybody said so.

Winter was hard on the old pump and hard on the people who had to come for water. After a full pail was removed from the spout, a few drops of water still fell and soon a mound of ice formed. When there was no more room beneath the spout to allow a pail to hang straight, Daddy came out of his office with a little hatchet and chopped the mound away.

Oftentimes the pump froze solid, but Daddy had a teakettle on his coal-burning space heater in the office. People could go to the office for the hot water and pour it over the pump to thaw it out. When the pump needed to be primed, again the kettle of water solved that problem.

There were only two or three times that I can remember someone pumping up a dead mouse.

Sometimes people tried to force the pump handle when it was frozen solid, and it often broke in two, leaving Daddy to buy a new one. Then again, a good farmer gave Daddy a five-spot now and then to help defray the cost of upkeep.

The well was also an important social center. At our house, when the pail was long gone from its place on the corner of the sink, we could be certain that whoever was getting the water had met someone at the well.

Important issues of the day were discussed at the pump. Information was passed on about an interesting new product now available at the general store, the price of eggs, and the coming event to be held in the city hall.

Here we learned that the school board had invited all the teachers to return for the next term, who was "in the family way," what variety of tomatoes was best to plant, and that Lois Somers came late to her own bridal shower.

Yes, the town pump was an important mainstay in our small-town way of life. ❖

The Park Bench

By Art Gardner

More years ago than I care to look back at, I worked in an office building near Columbus Circle in New York City. When the weather was nice, I would grab a sandwich and a cup of coffee at the Automat andspend the rest of my lunch hour strolling in Central Park. The park was not then at all what it has since become. The benches usually bore some prosperous-looking idlers—nursemaids with baby carriages, now and then a pair of grandfathers playing checkers or dominoes.

There was one bench in particular where I would sit awhile if there was time to spare. It was under a huge old maple on a slight rise near one of the exits and spread a welcome shade at midday.

I found it a delightful spot to watch the passing parade. Half-grown boys and girls sauntered by, sometimes hand in hand. Old-fashioned hansom cabs plodded along, bearing their quota of gaping tourists. I would get a kick out of the dog walkers, struggling to keep their charges moving on, stopping occasionally to untangle the leashes of as many as eight or nine pooches of assorted sizes and all manner of breeds and pedigrees. Sometimes a serious bicyclist would pedal past, glad to escape the fumes of Central Park West, nothing like what they are today but still an unpleasant contrast to the smell of freshly mowed grass and the flowering shrubs masking the exit.

Marie Dressler and Lillian Russell rode their bikes past here every day when they were not on tour. Someone told them to lose weight.

Once in a while I had company. An elderly codger might be sitting on the bench or would drop down next to me to pass the time of day. His ruddy complexion could only have been acquired by a man who had put in a lot of years outdoors. His eyes were as blue as Central Park's lake on a rare day in June. A white walrus mustache adorned his upper lip and a fringe of grayish white straggled out from under his old felt hat. When I saw him for the first time, I could picture him as one of New York's finest, a leftover from a previous generation, helmet cocked atop the back of his head, long-tailed, brass-buttoned gray coat, nightstick and all.

One sunny day in late spring, he caught me humming to myself: "While strolling through the park one day, in the merry month of May." He broke out in a hearty grin. "Sure," he chuckled, "and it's just such a day, my old granddad told me, the swells of little old New York would take the air hereabouts.

"I was 40 years on the force," he went on. "Well do I remember seeing Muggsy McGraw and Matty the Bix Six argue on this very bench how to pitch to Johnny Evers and Tinker and Chance. George M. Cohan would hire a cab and drive along this road. Many a time Ethel Barrymore and Lionel would be out in a fancy carriage, taking in the fresh air and soaking in the bright sunshine. Never Jack, though; he lived for the limelight and the footlights. You'd never catch him out in broad daylight."

I ventured, "I guess this battered old bench has seen a lot of strange things and held some very odd people."

"You can say that again. Marie Dressler and Lillian Russell rode their bikes past here every day when they were not on tour. Someone told them to lose weight. Buxom colleens were going out of style. The trouble was they'd get up such an appetite they'd order a full-course dinner for lunch."

He paused, then pointed to an old carving in the top rail of the bench back. "See these initials—J.B.B.? They were dug in by Big Jim himself. Ould Mike often spoke of him, togged out in a light green, wide-checked jacket and knickers, sporting a cap to match. Lots of times he would be piloting a three-wheeler, flashing his diamond transportation set. The stickpin would shine like the headlight on one of the locomotives so close to his heart. And there'd be Lillian, perched on the next seat like a queen. What a sight she'd be in her white serge suit, with leg-of-mutton sleeves, a bright green Tyrolean hat tilted over one eye and sitting on her golden-blond hair like a crown. On the rear seat would toil the bike valet, pumping with all his might to earn the princely salary of twinty bucks a week. And, d'you know, belike they'd stop at this very bench and finish off a gallon of orange juice the valet squeezed that morning.

"A foin picture they made. In those days the park was no way uptown. You can bet no crook came within a block of Jim. Every man on the force was his friend, not only because they were Irish, too, but any cop who did Jim a favor could count on a sawbuck at Christmas or a fiver when riding with him out of the park."

With that, he got to his feet and sauntered out of Olmstead's playground with me, shaking his head and leaving the bench, sadly in need of a coat of paint, to accumulate new memories. ❖

All Hail the Trolley Man

By Robert Harris

Firemen and policemen rode free on the trolleys— and they never sat down. Instead, they stood up front with the motorman and talked like old friends. (This was the reason most boys wanted to be one or the other when they grew up.)

In the winter, factory whistles didn't blow until it was nearly dark. The cars were crowded with men carrying lunch boxes and reading papers. The lights were turned on, and if it was cold out the windows frosted over.

In addition to their regular duties, the conductor and motorman were expected to assist the police and the fire department. They stopped runaway horses, assisted elderly and disabled passengers, handled the drunks, prevented cruelty to animals and were always courteous to a blasé and uncaring public. Most important, motormen had an uncanny knack for spotting lost children.

A network of cords, rods and signal wires ran above the passengers' heads for the entire length of the car. The conductor signaled the motorman when passengers were safely on or off. A double ring of the bell signified all-clear. He also rang up the fares on a dial at one end of the car in full view of the passengers or the occasional inspector.

Passengers could request a transfer entitling them to ride another car to a different part of the city. Conductors punched the transfer with a half-hour leeway, but often this was not enough time, as some of the cars did not run that often. However, an argument with the conductor usually ended in the passenger's favor.

In autumn, the leaves fell thickly on the pavement. The cold rain soaked them and formed a thick, insulating pad on the tracks. When the steel wheels ground them to pulp, there were great orange and blue flames and the sharp smell of ozone.

Occasionally the trolley company had problems with honesty among employees. A standard joke on the vaudeville circuits concerned the conductor who tossed all the coins taken in up into the air. Those that landed on their edges belonged to the company. This conductor usually was named "Rob Nichols."

During rush hours, aisles were crowded with standing men and women. Each seat had a brass handle on its aisle side for standees, and in a few places, straps hung from an overhead pipe. Each time the car stopped to take on passengers, the conductor shouted, "Please step forward in the aisle!"

In no way could the standees move, and each head swiveled around like a horse with blinders to look at the conductor in astonishment. The conductor knew as well as they that no movement was possible.

> *They stopped runaway horses, assisted elderly and disabled passengers, handled the drunks, prevented cruelty to animals and were always courteous to a blasé and uncaring public.*

On cold winter days a horse falling on the tracks or a truck with solid rubber tires caught in the deep icy ruts along the tracks caused tie-ups of 10 or 12 cars while everyone waited for a solution. One soon learned not to speak to people whose ears were white-tipped. One didn't ask if they had to wait long for the trolley; it was dangerous to talk to such people.

On Sundays, our father took us on a trolley ride to the end of the line and back again. (I now realize that my father did this to get us out of Mother's hair while she made Sunday dinner.) We usually had the entire car to ourselves, and the seat backs could be swung so the rider could face in either direction.

Sometimes we stood up near the motorman to watch him run the car. The top of the control was marked off in segments corresponding to different speeds. Next to the large handle that controlled the speed was a smaller handle, the reverse. To the right of the control box and set in a maze of small pipes was the brake lever. It was tricky, and no motorman would ever impart to any child the intricacies of its operation. One could stand and watch for hours and never be really sure (if some emergency arose where he *had* to take over for the motorman) how to stop the car.

The cars went faster on Sundays. There wasn't much traffic and they didn't have to stop so often for passengers. The stores were closed and the streets were still. Once out of the business area, the car picked up speed. The buildings changed to soot-covered factories with blackened windows. Cranes with large hooks hung motionless in the still air.

Soon the factories gave way to houses without lawns or gardens, with trash and lumber piled high in the yards. Suddenly we were out of the city. The car slowed to cross a switch onto a single track. The rails were now spiked to ties just like the rails for trains. The car successfully crossed the switch, "dusted off its hands" and started the remainder of the run. The motorman placed the control lever at full speed and the car gathered momentum.

We were now cruising at a breathtaking 25 miles an hour. Tall country grasses, buttercups and daisies waved in the breeze. Red-winged blackbirds flew from tree to wire. Black-and-white cows gazed over barbed-wire fences. The faint odor of cow manure was alien to our nostrils; we thought it was the odor of fresh air.

We were at the end of the line.

Gone was the magic. The motorman and conductor suddenly became plain men. The return trip was like seeing a movie a second time, so we amused ourselves with games like, "There's a dead skunk in the road, I one it." The next player said, "I two it," and so on until it came to the player who had to say, "I ate it." That's the end of the game, and the raucous laughter was always out of proportion to the humor.

As we approached our corner, our father reached up and rang the bell. The car stopped and, in silence, we got off, glad to be home and knowing that in a few minutes we would sit down to a good meal. All except the baby; she wanted to stay on the car, so our father carried her, screaming, to the pavement. The conductor gave a double pull on his bell cord and the trolley rolled away toward the other end of the line. ❖

JAY KILLIAN

Shave and a Haircut, Six Bits

By Fletcher Croom

Today's child undergoing her weekly or biweekly trip to the beauty shop for a haircut would not possibly have as fascinating or entertaining a time as I did on my monthly or bimonthly trip to Mr. Ake's barbershop.

Of great interest to me was the shop, with its three chairs that mysteriously went up and down when Mr. Ake pumped something behind me as I sat down. Clutched by the hand of my parent, I would be led into the shop, and we took from a square board on the wall a metal number that was attached to a hook of monstrous proportions. Ten or 12 numbers hung there, and they proclaimed at what stage of Mr. Ake's day you might have your turn at Mr. Ake's shears and clippers. If we were early, we might be No. 2 and would sit in the captain's chairs lining the wall. If we were No. 9, my mother might go on down the street to the grocery, or even go home and return in time for my turn, her time mysteriously calculated by a formula of Mr. Ake's that never failed.

When our number was called, we carefully replaced the number on the hook, and I then climbed into the chair and was sent soaring upward to meet Mr. Ake's face on a level with mine.

Mr. Ake enveloped me in a huge sheet of cloth, pinned tightly at the back of my neck. Mother and Mr. Ake discussed how I was to have my hair cut. It never occurred to either of them to ask me what I would like. Only once did I venture an opinion. I longed for some fat sausage curls hanging around my shoulders. So convinced was I of Mr. Ake's skill that once I timidly asked for a longer cut necessary for such a coiffure. "Nonsense," chorused my mother and Mr. Ake and returned to their discussion.

Usually my hair was to be cut just below my ears in a straight line and straight across my forehead in bangs, since there was little else that could be done with fine, straight hair such as mine—at least, little else that Mr. Ake knew about.

As the shears went *snip-snap,* I would cringe a little, bringing a soft rebuke from my mother. "Sit still, or you might be nipped on the ear."

But sit still I could not, and Mr. Ake deftly avoided my ears. I can't remember a single time he ever nipped me, although I heard gory tales of restless children whose blood poured onto the pristine whiteness of the covering cloth.

The really difficult time for me came when the clippers were used. They were hand operated, always seemed to be in need of sharpening, and pulled at the hairs on the back of my neck until sometimes I squeezed out a tear or two.

Finally Mr. Ake used a soft brush sprinkled with a sweet-smelling white powder to whisk away the fuzz from my shoulders and face, and stood

> *When our number was called, I then climbed into the chair and was sent soaring upward to meet Mr. Ake's face on a level with mine.*

back to survey his work, with critical analysis from my mother. "Perhaps it should be a little shorter?" she would ask. After all, a haircut must last several weeks. He would grudgingly agree and snip off an infinitesimal bit around my ears.

Then I would be lifted down from the chair, my dress straightened and off we went through the screen door of the shop, not to return for six or eight weeks.

Sometimes, when my mother had errands to run that she could do more quickly without my tagging at her heels, she would seat me in one of the huge chairs and tell me to stay until Mr. Ake called my name. She would entrust me with the number, which I held tightly until he called for me.

Sitting quietly, my short legs sticking out in front of me, I observed all the strange activities in the world of men. Some men would be shaved, and each had a special mug with his name on it on a shelf beside the enormous mirror behind the barber chairs. The barber stirred up a rich lather and painted it all over the man's face with a small brush. The customer reclined, swathed in the same sort of white cloth that enveloped me for a haircut. The difference was that the cloth came only to his lap while I was completely covered, tips of shoes and all.

When the lather was thick enough for his satisfaction, Mr. Ake picked up a murderous-looking knife and slapped it back and forth on a black strap until its sharpness suited him. With long and artful strokes he could cut into the lather on the man's face, leaving a path that showed only skin where he had scraped. Then he would wipe his razor on a towel attached to the back of the chair and proceed to scrape another path.

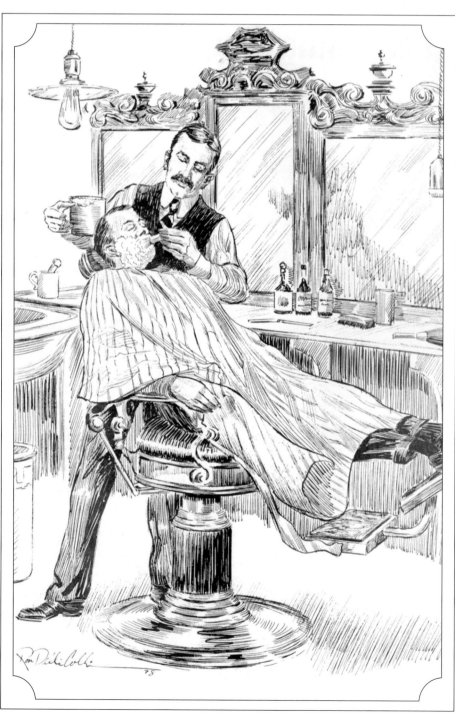

I wondered how he knew where to start, but he always finished with a clean-shaven face.

Some men had a preshave treatment of hot towels, wrung out and wrapped around the man's face until only his nose poked out. The towels were left in place until they cooled and then were exchanged for fresh hot ones. The men never seemed to mind the heat, but I writhed sometimes watching the steam arising from the freshly applied towels. It did not seem to bother these huge men with lots of loud talk and jocular stories and slappings of the knee.

Occasionally during a story, Mr. Ake would raise his eyebrows significantly and nod toward me, sitting there all eyes and ears. The customer would stop abruptly, hesitate, change his tone of voice, and continue his story after polishing his language a little. But at other times, his voice would drop to such a low murmur that even Mr. Ake had to lean forward to hear the continued story. How I did wish for more acuity!

Often the men, all friends of my father, would joke with me. Sometimes they would present me with a stick of chewing gum, which I would hold, along with the number, until my mother returned and gave me permission to chew it.

At the end of the shave, Mr. Ake would splash a spicy-smelling liquid on his hands. He rubbed his hands briskly together and applied the bay rum to the man's pink skin, slapping it smartly. Then he would raise the man to a sitting position, and the customer would run his hands over his clean-shaven face.

The most fascinating part of the shop was strictly forbidden to me, and I often stared at the limp cretonne curtains that hung on a tightly stretched string over an opening in the wall. Near the curtain hung a sign that I did not learn to read until I was in the first grade: "Baths, 25 cents; with soap, 30 cents." I knew the numbers, but had no idea what went on behind that curtain.

The most fascinating part of the shop was strictly forbidden to me, and I often stared at the limp cretonne curtains that hung on a tightly stretched string over an opening in the wall.

I watched the lean-hipped, big-hatted, booted men come in from the ranches. They joked with the barbers and any other men in the shop. Then they would order "The works!" and disappear behind the curtain. Strange sounds of water and sputterings would come from behind the curtains, and sometimes a burst of song. It was all very puzzling until I was able to spell out the letters of the sign.

The cowboys would appear from behind the curtains, rosy, in fresh clothes, although I never did figure out what they did with their soiled ones. They probably left them in a heap on the floor until the laundry sent over for them. Sometimes clouds of steam poured from behind the curtains, making the space there seem a sorcerer's palace where the dirty, tired men were refreshed into the gay and gallant figures they appeared to be.

Then they would seat themselves in the barber's chair for a shave and haircut. While this took place, the one black man of the town would work over the boots on the outstretched feet, polishing and cleaning, snapping his taut cloth over the toes for a high-gloss finish. As the cowboy rose in glory from the barber chair, he would flip a dime to the shoe polisher, who always caught it with an accurate movement of his hand, flashing a wide smile at this customer.

Sometimes the cowboy would fish in his pocket and laboriously count out his 75 cents for the barber, but at other times he would say offhandedly, "Put it on the cuff, OK?" Mr. Ake would go to the cash register, find a wrinkled paper and, with a pencil stump, write hieroglyphics only he understood.

Then my name might be called, or my mother might return from her errands. I always left regretfully, but with many sights and sounds to puzzle about until my return next month or the month after. ❖

My First Permanent Wave

By Helen Daley

Living in a small Colorado town, we didn't have any beauty parlor or shops until the early '20s. We wore our hair in long braids until our midteens, when we were permitted to "put our hair up," denoting a growing-up milestone (just as the boys had to wear knee pants until they were deemed old enough to wear long pants).

Ear puffs became the fad. We'd rat or tease our hair on the side and in front, and if it was thin, we'd put "rats" (balls of hair) inside and pin it up. The bigger the puffs, the more fashionable we thought we were.

In the back, a round bun would take care of the hair. Some girls with curly hair would make curls that fell down over the bun, and it was quite pretty. Bangs were popular, sometimes tied down in front with a favorite pretty ribbon. The boys always reminded us that we had to do that to tie in our brains.

Most every household had a curling iron. We let the wooden handles rest on the top of a lamp chimney with the iron above the flame and the flame turned low. When we thought it was hot enough, we'd test it either by using some hair combings or by wetting a finger and quickly touching the iron. If it sputtered, it was just right. Sometimes the iron would be too hot and then we'd have a hunk of burned or singed hair.

Sometimes the iron would be too hot and then we'd have a hunk of burned or singed hair.

For curlers, there were the "kid" curlers, a pliable wire with a piece of cotton around it, encased in a piece of soft kid leather about 5 inches long. It was pliable and could be bent back after the hair was wound around it.

Later, when bobbed hair came in, many condemned it as a sign of loose character, but gradually it was accepted and became quite common. Eventually the "shingle" in back was popular. We had to go into a man's barbershop for our bobs, and it was with daring boldness that we entered with several girlfriends, curious yet fearful.

A marcel iron for home use came on the market, but wasn't always successful. It was a wide iron with several fluted grooves, and it was heated and your hair placed in the grooves. Then, as it was waved, you brought it down the strand of hair until you got as much wave as you wanted. It was too wide to heat in the ordinary lamp chimney, so we used the cookstove.

Then a lady took a course in Denver and opened a beauty shoppe. She cut hair, shampooed and marcelled it. They heated long curling irons that had a long, curved blade which fit over the rod partway around. The operator would heat these, then put around a strand of hair, pull gently, and wind and heat till she thought it was curled. Then, on to the next strand, pulling it a bit differently so the hair was waved in deep waves. When we were finished, we really felt dressed up. Of course, few of us could afford to have that done, as it was considered a real luxury.

Then came the permanent waves. I vividly recall my first. Having a chance to spend the day in the big city of Denver, I went to a beauty school where prices were greatly reduced. These girls were finishing their beauty course and needed the final practice with an overseer.

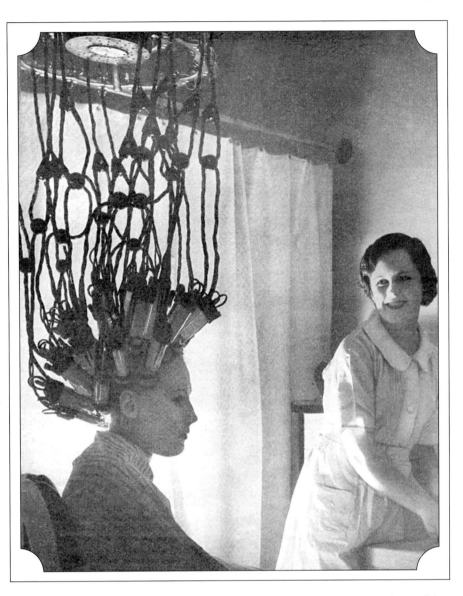

The machine was a huge thing made of metal, with long wires hanging down with clamps on the ends of the wires. I had to sit quite awhile as the operator rolled my hair on some gadgets, then put a clamp on the end of each curl. By the time my hair was all rolled and clamped, my head felt pretty top-heavy.

Then came the frightening experience of "cooking" or "steaming." The heat was turned on, and while the girl had put lots of pieces of cotton under each clamp, sometimes there'd be a spot that would get hot and burn my scalp. I sure didn't move around, as I might get steamed. From time to time, a test curl would be examined, and when finally it was thought my hair had "taken," the electricity was turned off and we waited till the metal was cool enough to handle. All the paraphernalia was removed. My head felt so relieved to lose that heavy load. My hair was a mass of kinky curls. Then it was set. As a rule, most would shampoo and set their hair themselves after that. The machine permanent took much longer.

We would get to have our hair fixed for a special event like a junior-senior banquet or graduation, and what a thrill to have an appointment with the hairdresser! Now it seems quite commonplace, but I still can remember the thrill of my first permanent wave many years ago. ❖

"Hello Girl" of World War I

By Nell Owen

In 1916, I went to work for Southern Indiana Bell Telephone Company at Chrisney, Ind. I worked the noon hour and the evening hours, 6–9 p.m.; the other hours were worked by Beatrice Bench. It was a one-switchboard office, so we were both local and long-distance operators. All telephone numbers were on the board, and when a customer called, a "drop" fell and we plugged in using the answer cord and said, "Operator."

We needed to know all telephone numbers, all nicknames, how to spell all words, and the names of all members in a family.

When they gave the number they wanted, we plugged in the ringing cord to the number and rang. These cords were attached to the board and we rang by pressing a small lever. Each customer had a certain ring, one long for private lines and a different number of rings for party lines. We operators wore headphones attached to the board so we could hear. But we were instructed not to "listen in" on conversations or we would lose our jobs.

Beatie wore braces that fastened to her shoes and supported her legs to above her knees. It was a birth defect, but she learned to live with it, and how wonderfully she managed! The one-room office was upstairs in the Masonic building. She left her crutches at the bottom of the stairs and crawled up to the switchboard.

We operators were "watch dogs" for all accidents or any other news that the customers wanted. We needed to know all telephone numbers, all nicknames, how to spell all words, and the names of all members in a family (both near and distant). If someone was ill, we were called to ask if the doctor had been called and which doctor. Operators in those days really belonged to their customers.

One customer, a businessman, called an Indianapolis wholesale house. When he rang, we answered, and he always said, "Give me Indianapolis," and hung up. We had to call back and ask him whom he wanted. Then we were really "told off." He would say, "Don't be so dumb. You know who I want!" and he hung up again.

We did know, because we kept the Indianapolis number and address handy. We called him back each time so we could giggle when he called us "dumb." He was a kind and gentle person and would never have called us "dumb" away from the switchboard.

All lines in the country were party lines and each customer had a certain ring—one or two long and some short ones. The hard part of getting a call through was people taking the receivers down to listen in, because this weakened the ring. Each telephone on a party line received all rings, but were supposed to answer only their ring. This seldom happened, because they answered any ring they wanted to and they wanted to most of the time.

Somebody usually came on and said, "They aren't home. I think they are at her mother's or gone to town, because I saw them going someplace." If the party-line customer knew the ringee, the call wasn't wasted, because they had a visit via telephone.

One man, when his ring came, took down his receiver and waited a few seconds; then he said, "Is everybody ready?" He said that it made him so mad when they came in on his calls.

One time I couldn't get a call through, so I said, "Lucy, get off the line."

A few days later I saw her, and she said, "Nell, how did you know I was on the line?"

I told her that I knew her clock tick. She laughed and said that she would have to stop her clock. Operators did learn certain sounds in the homes.

The heartache of putting through a death call and the joy of ringing for happy news made an operator feel close to the customer and part of a big family.

I was Miss Columbia and Roscoe Harrell was Uncle Sam for Chrisney during the war. We went to schools for flag raisings and to sell Liberty Bonds. Roscoe's wife, Bess, took our picture and sent it overseas to her cousin in the Army. It was put in an overseas paper, and I got a lot of letters from homesick GIs. They called me their "Hello Girl."

During the 1918 flu epidemic, Beatie and I kept watch at the switchboard 24 hours each day. We couldn't "close" the board at night, as we usually did, because a doctor might be needed. So many operators were ill that chief operators and male supervisors from Rockport, Ind., were filling in where needed. When I got the flu, Beatie and one of our linemen would answer a ring by saying, "This is your beautiful operator."

Being a "Hello Girl" has given me a lot of happy memories and a love for Indiana Bell Telephone Company. ❖

Small-Town Bank

By Walt Messenger

It was 1917. I had been knocked out of college by polio. When I was able to get around on crutches, I heard that the local National Bank needed another employee. After a couple of interviews, I got the job. There were already three people working there; I was No. 4. The cashier ran things, and there was an assistant who held the job because of his reputation as a sound businessman. Then there was George, who really did most of the actual work. The bank president ran another business and only dropped in to check up on things.

Salaries in those days ranged from the $2,000 per year the cashier received to the $30 per month I started with. The assistant cashier and George each got $75 per month. Before I left to return to college, my pay went up to $45 per month.

As last man on the job, I was also janitor. That meant tending the coal-fired furnace, sweeping the walks and the bank floor, washing windows and scrubbing the white tile floor. The latter was a problem, for just as sure as I got it all spick-and-span, a farmer would come in to bank a large milk check; said farmer chewed tobacco and he spit whenever needed, no matter.

> *Salaries in those days ranged from the $2,000 per year the cashier received to the $30 per month I started with.*

George called his attention to the nice clean tile one day. "Oh, I'm sorry," he replied—and a minute or two later added to the mess.

The greater part of our work was done by hand. While we had an adding machine, we used it mostly to total long columns. We also had a Burrough's bookkeeping machine for posting the customer ledger sheets and statement sheets. One typewriter was available for writing letters.

Banks had their problem customers in those days, but as we knew all of them personally, we were able to deal with them. There was an auto dealer who would go to Buffalo and get new cars, give them a check, then wait for us to call him when the check came in. In that way, he saved a few days' interest. The cashier did not like it, but tolerated it. One time, when the cashier was away and the big check came in, George had me protest it. We lost the man's account for about three months; then he was back, and more careful.

Bank examiners always frowned on over-drafts in those days and we tried to keep them to a minimum. I wrote the overdrawing customer a letter, requesting him to make a deposit to cover. Once I got exceptionally quick action. The man was 56 cents overdrawn, but in typing the letter, I got the period on the wrong side of the 56. He rushed in from his country home, shouting that someone had raised a check on him. I got called on that one, but when the man admitted that he knew he was overdrawn for a few cents, the cashier remarked that maybe I had a good idea for getting fast action.

Then there was the case of a woman who took over her husband's business when he was sick. In less than a week, she had his account overdrawn for a substantial amount.

I wrote the usual letter. Wow! She came in raving about how she knew banks had to make money, but did they have to pick on a woman with a sick husband?

I made out a new statement and the cashier called on the lady that evening. The story was that when she received our regular monthly statement, she saw that our balance was larger than the one in her checkbook, so she crossed out the checkbook balance and took ours, disregarding the fact that numerous checks had been sent out that were not back to the bank yet.

Not all troubles were from customers. One morning the vault would not open. We first thought that the time clock had been overwound. A local doctor applied his stethoscope to the door but could not hear a clock ticking. Meanwhile, a hasty run was made to another bank where $12,000 was borrowed so we could do business, and we used scrap paper for bookkeeping.

A hasty call was put in to the lock makers. The first question they asked was, "What do you oil the bolts with?" When we mentioned a well-advertised oil, they informed us that the oil we were using had a tendency to get gummy and that was probably our trouble. They suggested setting the combination for unlocking, then taking a heavy timber and pounding on the door. It worked. Then we cleaned the bolts and used a lubricant they recommended.

A few other incidents stick to my memory. Two men were partners in a lumbering business, one well along in years, thrifty and dependable, and the other much younger who liked to be a big shot. He rented a big house, dressed in the latest style and was a free spender. He maintained three bank accounts in three towns. Whenever his account was low in our bank, he deposited a check on one of the other banks. We suspected he was kiting checks, so we sent one directly to the bank he

had used and it came back "no funds." That stopped that practice.

A woman who apparently had little experience with money presented a $50 check one day. Asked how she would like it, she said, "Oh, give me two 25s."

The assistant cashier replied, "We're fresh out of 25s. How about two 20s and a 10?"

That was all right with her.

Then there was the professional man who was paying for a house. He decided to hurry things up a bit and came in and told us to buy some Studebaker stock—it was $17 that day. We did and he took the certificate. Every day after that he came in to find out the price of that stock, and because it was just a bit lower than his cost, he became worried. Finally, when it hit $17, he said, "Sell it. I'm tired of losing sleep."

The teller bought it, held it fewer than 30 days, and sold it at a profit.

The president of the bank came in one day and ordered 100 shares of a certain oil stock. The next time he came in, the cashier told him he had the bill—$4,000.

He jumped. "I thought that stock was $4 a share!" He grabbed the *Wall Street Journal*. It had gone up in three days to $80 a share. "Sell," he said, and the result was a nice profit—on a mistake.

One day when I was posting the

statements, for some reason I could never figure out, I questioned the signature on a check issued by the brother of the assistant cashier, a lumberman. It was a good-size check, so I took it to the cashier. He compared it to the man's signature cards and said it looked all right. We showed it to the man's brother; he, too, said it looked like Ted's signature, but he would soon find out, and he reached for the telephone.

When he hung up, he chuckled. Ted said he had done a lot of heavy work that day and his hand was so shaky he couldn't write. He had had the man make out the check and he had him copy his signature from another check, but anyway the check was to be paid.

On Saturday morning, we made up a payroll for an acid factory in a small neighboring community. I took the package to the O & W Express office at noon, got the receipt and put it in my pocket. Usually I took it to the bank Monday morning.

On this day, I followed the usual procedure. Also, on this particular Saturday, Dad wanted to visit a small place nearby, and as I was the family driver, we left early. Meanwhile, there were frantic calls from the factory and attempts to find me. All came out all right when the factory manager found the expressman, a substitute, who had concluded that a Monday delivery would be all right and had put the package in the office safe.

And that reminds me of another incident. I had not been on the job too long when one morning, while sweeping the floor, I found a $5 bill. I shoved it in my pocket, and when the cashier came in, I took it to him and remarked, "Someone was getting careless with money." It was 20 years later when it came to me that the five-spot had been planted to see what I would do about it.

In those days, national banks issued their own bank notes, 10s and 20s, as I recall. The government sent them to us in sheets of four.

It was 20 years later when it came to me that the five-spot had been planted to see what I would do about it.

My job was to stamp the president's and cashier's names on them and cut them apart. We would get a new lot when the old ones were returned to Washington in worn-out condition.

Those were the days of World War I. We sold Liberty Loan Bonds and War Savings Stamps. That increased our workload without adding anything to the profits. Our rules required us to balance the books before we went home at night. When they failed to balance, George would ask me if I had done any subtracting that day, a weak point in my mathematics. I would always remember such things and the point was easily cleared up. On the other hand, it was harder to check the work of the elderly assistant cashier because he could not remember all the items that passed through his hands. In fact, when he was on vacation, we closed up an hour earlier.

During the war, a farmer wanted to close out his account and asked for gold. George finally talked him out of it. We had gold coins that usually went out just before Christmas and were back in by New Year's. For the fun of it, I once cashed an $8 check of my own in silver dollars, then went out and presented them in the local stores. They were all back within a few days.

Bank examiners did not bother us much. They would frown on any overdrafts—we always seemed to get more just before the examiners arrived. They might question us about a few loans that had run longer than they considered wise, but we knew the borrowers and maintained they were all right.

Years later, I had a visit with the over-90-year-old cashier who was still working and asked him how they made out during the time of bank closings. He admitted that the examiners had him worried, but they survived. He added that, from what he knew, about half the banks that the government closed were in good condition and should not have been forced to close. ❖

Down to the Depot

By Leola V. Kester

In this day of air and highway traffic, the railway depot is almost a thing of the past. I have seen many deserted small-town depots sitting in a dilapidated state, surrounded by weeds—a fit subject for a wandering artist, but for nothing else! Not long ago, I visited one that had been converted into a museum. Certainly it was more fortunate than most!

When I was a girl, the depot, or "the station," as it was called in some communities, was an important hub of local commerce. There the farmer with his "rig" waited for freight from the city, and the merchant waited with his truck to pick up stock for his store. There, also, the town's unemployed sat at train time, for want of something better to do.

We stood on the platform, watching the huge steam engine with its one eye and shrill wailing whistle as it approached along the weed-strewn track.

My friends and I made frequent pilgrimages there, too. We stood on the platform, watching the huge steam engine with its one eye and shrill wailing whistle as it approached along the weed-strewn track. We shivered with awe as it came closer, and as the noise became deafening, we covered our ears with our hands and willed ourselves to stand rooted to the spot, although our timid inner selves wanted to turn and run! (I feel the same way today at an airport!)

But what fantasies that train inspired! It was only a local—a few freight cars and one lone passenger coach—but as we watched the stationmaster come out to accept a few cartons of unknown merchandise, the brakeman inspect the wheels, and the conductor help the passengers to dismount, we dreamed of the time when we would embark on such a journey!

Sometimes we did actually take the train to the nearest town to spend the day shopping and perhaps to see a movie, returning late in the afternoon, tired but happy! Those were real occasions, and I can still hear the ringing of the bell as we departed and feel and smell the ancient plush seats as we got under motion.

The whistle shrieked a warning as we neared the crossing just outside town, and we watched one or two autos wait for us to go by. The trip, only 4 miles, was all too short; yet we were anxious to get to town, perhaps to buy a new hat, or material for a summer dress.

On other days we just watched the train go by and snooped around the station and the dusty waiting room until the stationmaster told us we'd better go home now.

As I grew older, we walked the tracks to our favorite swimming hole under the railroad tracks. We took the tracks for two reasons: It was the shortest route; and we were ashamed to be seen on the street in our old raincoats, which Mama insisted we wear, even on the hottest day! Of course, in those days, no one appeared on the street in a bathing suit! That was unheard of, even though they covered more than our "street clothes" do now! It was even worse coming back, walking in wet suits—the "portable steam bath"! By the time we got home, we needed a bath to cool off again.

But it was lots of fun there in the cool water in the shadow of the iron bridge. While we were swimming, we sometimes saw a train cross the bridge. The engineer waved and we waved back.

I remember the first time I went to a town where there was a mainline road, and the trains ran all night! The sound of that lonesome whistle thrilled me, but made me snuggle deeper into the bed. Once I got brave and looked out to see sparks and fire shooting out of the stack, with a tail like a comet!

Now I am older, and most of the trains, as well as the depots, are gone from this part of the country. But I still love them. One of the most enjoyable trips I ever took was to West Virginia in 1960 via the Phoebe Snow, the Pennsylvania, and the C & O. And I'll never forget that huge Washington, D.C., terminal where I almost got lost! I guess you could put all of the small-town depots in Pennsylvania in it!

As you see, I still love to go "down to the depot." I hope to take another train somewhere before I die! ❖

JAY KILLIAN

Service Station Brat

By Doris Allen

After turning onto Jackson Road, the rickety school bus chugged and swayed for 2 miles before sputtering to a halt. A lush green holly tree waved to me through the smudged window. Its red berries signaled I was home.

I stepped away from the clamor and stench of the afternoon bus and welcomed fresh country air. The stately brick house framed by the pines of the Community Forest was inviting, but that wasn't my first stop. I ran across the pebble drive to Daddy's service station.

Shielding my eyes from the sun, I squinted between my fingers to view the overhead sign. It stood like a giant sheriff protecting the small frame building. An enormous red star within a white circle supported the word "TEXACO."

The gas pumps were like three prim grandmothers promenading in long dresses. Rubber hoses on the left were their walking canes, gently tapping the ground. Turn the flour-sifter handles on the right and the ladies started to hum. Ethel, Indian and Regular had globe faces and wore pungent perfume.

A mockingbird and a blue jay argued in the pecan orchard as I skipped across the concrete slab toward the front step. The freshly cleaned windows smelled of diluted ammonia. As I entered, I read the handwritten sign under the buzzer: "Ring Bell For Service."

Tires, batteries and other car parts filled the entire right half of the room, creating a rubbery musk odor. On the left, a long counter stretched to midroom, separating front from back. I tiptoed to see over it into the office area. The walls were neatly lined with shelves and drawers, all painted to match the kelly green of the counter. Intermittent news and static spouted from the box radio sitting on top of the desk near the back door. An electric fan hummed, oscillating as if watching a tennis match in slow motion.

The wooden floor gave a slight bounce as I bounded across to the glass candy case.

Butterfinger, Baby Ruth and Hershey chocolate bars lined the shelves. Lollipops and peanuts were stored in Planter's jars on the counter. Next to the candy case, a red oblong cooler displayed the white script words "Coca-Cola." Its top doors slid open to reveal soda pop so cold that frosty slush had formed in each bottle. The cardboard sign tacked to the wall read, "Drinks and Candy—5 cents each."

I scanned the comic book shelf on my way out. The concrete grease ramps were like two huge magnets drawing me toward them. I sashayed up one sloped side, leaped across the blackened oil pit and walked smugly down the other.

I ran around the station, past the back-to-back rest rooms, then followed the stepping stones toward home.

When the new highway was built, it bypassed the station. Business dwindled and the building was torn down. Two flowering mimosa trees were planted on the vacant ground, but they were never as beautiful as the memories I hold of Daddy's service station. ❖

Free Outdoor Movies

By Lucille Kleist

With a flick of the finger and for a small fee, the video disk player will bring the latest movies right into your family room. You don't even have to stand in line to buy tickets. It's a far cry from the free outdoor movies of the '30s.

In those days, all the little towns around the countryside had a free outdoor movie. It was usually held in a vacant lot next to a tavern or grocery store. Older people sat on wooden planks held up by huge chunks of wood, while the younger kids stood, giggling teen-age girls standing in the arms of gangly half-grown boys.

I remember those days especially well because my dad, L.T. Packard, made free movie night something to be remembered for years to come. When Dad bought his 40 acres halfway between Portage and Poynette, Wis., on Highway 51, he started his own little empire that he called "Packardville."

Sundays at Packardville started early for the family and friends, usually by 4 a.m. The excitement and anticipation of the day chased all sleep away.

There were many things to be attended to at this early Sunday-morning hour and L.T. was ready to delegate duties to every one of us. Empty cigar boxes were lined up in rows on the dining-room table, waiting their share of the copper pennies, shiny silver and crisp bills that Dad counted into each. They held exactly $20, to be used in making change for nickel ice-cream cones and 10-cent bottles of orange soda.

There were pounds of golden butter to melt and pour into the huge granite coffeepot, later to be poured over the white popcorn. Tubs of crystal ice were filled with glass bottles of soda. Hamburger was made into pats, wieners were clipped at the joints and the ice-cream man carried in canvas-covered cartons holding dry ice, packed around tempting tubs of butterpecan, dark brown chocolate and berry-filled pink ice cream.

Tiny flags, medium flags and large flags decorated every stand and every post. Dad was a patriotic man.

Fresh white sand was dumped under the playground slides and swings, perfect for the landing of tiny bare feet. Those were the days when shoes weren't always a necessity.

Finally all was ready and the day began. The carousel played, "Give me a June night, the moonlight and you in my arms." The man in the hamburger stand was calling out his wares and shouts of "Bingo!" filled the air. The softball game was started in the ballpark while ice-cream cones were dipped by the hundreds. Cold orange pop was guzzled and every stomach was so full that often picnic suppers were never touched.

Suddenly it was dusk, and the movie started. Tom Mix rode his horse as he chased Indians who were always trying to get away. As the movie ended and Mix kissed the heroine, one could hear giggles from the teen-agers cuddled together on the long rows of wooden planks.

Sometimes there would be a mammoth display of fireworks before the lights came on. At last the show was over, and the cars were loaded with tired kids and contented parents. When the last car headed for home, we carried the money and the supplies back to the house, shut off the lights and hid the day's cash gains in the cold-air registers.

Just before we fell asleep, we thought of Monday. Monday was another day to arise early. There was the park to rake, the paper to pick up, and maybe, if we were lucky, we'd find some coins in the debris. Some coins to use next Sunday on the carousel. ❖

Those
Saturday Movies

By Velma N. Tate

Whenever I pass a movie marquee advertising some super-film for $7, I remember the Good Old Days when 25 cents gave a kid an afternoon at the movies—transportation, entertainment and refreshments—and this small investment also gave our mothers a chance to do the Saturday cleaning and baking without having us underfoot.

In 1924, our family moved to a village called South Elgin, about 3 miles from the thriving town of Elgin, Ill., the city where they made all those watches. Coming from the country, my sister, age 9, and I, age 11, soon made friends with a large, jolly family named Ryan who lived just up the street. Geraldine Ryan and I became chums, and her younger sister, Ruth, and my sister, Rose Marie, were soon inseparable.

There was no rating system in those days, but our mothers had their own system, and the younger girls were sure to tattle if we saw a forbidden movie.

The four of us were soon spending all our Saturday afternoons in Elgin, which boasted three movie houses. As I recall, the two we patronized most were the Fox and the Grove. The Rialto, which had a real stage, cost more, but my father was an easy touch, and when extra nickels and dimes found their way from his pockets to ours, we would go there.

It was at the Rialto that I saw my first professional actors. They were called the Arthur Gale Players, and they must have been one of the last troupes in the Midwest. Their repertoire ranged from song-and-dance acts through stand-up comedy to "real plays," which held us spellbound.

We used to walk about a mile to catch the interurban trolley, whose official name was the Chicago-Aurora-Elgin Railroad. We called it the Third Rail, and believed that if we stepped on the extra rail, which carried electricity, we would be burnt instantly to little black cinders. I never knew anyone who was brave enough to try it. The Third Rail ran every half-hour, and being under 12, we rode for half-fare—5 cents.

At the end of the run, the conductor would get out and reverse the trolley, then slide the backs of the straw seats into reverse so that they faced forward for the return trip. I've often wondered why today's subway cars aren't designed on the same principle.

Lee Dubin

The Third Rail was always on time and was staffed by a motorman who did the driving and a conductor who collected the fares. By the time Geraldine and I started high school in Elgin two years later, we knew every motorman and conductor on the line, and I feel sure that if we had ever had any problems en route, they would have acted like kind uncles.

This is the great picture upon which the famous comedian has worked a whole year.

6 reels of Joy.

Charles Chaplin

IN

"THE KID"

Written and directed by Charles Chaplin

A First National ⊛ Attraction

We timed our arrival in Elgin early enough to do some window-shopping, since all of the movie houses were on Fountain Square, the main drag. (The city's first skyscraper was built there a few years later; I think it was about eight stories high.) We also allowed time to visit Woolworth's or Kresge's and invest in a nickel's

worth of candy apiece. Can you imagine what would happen nowadays if you asked for a nickel's worth of candy? In 1924, it bought a quarter-pound and we passed the bags back and forth throughout the program.

If we had any extra money, we did some comparison shopping before deciding on a purchase. In those days, everything in Woolworth's was actually priced at 5 or 10 cents. You could even buy silk stockings for a dime a stocking, or 20 cents a pair. Kresge's across the street had a five-and-dime store, and next-door was a 25-cent-to-$1 store known as "the Dollar Store." Our extra cash usually went to the jewelry department where we could buy a ring, bracelet, string of beads or earrings for 10 cents. A year or so later, we were investing heavily in cosmetics—to be applied after we left home for school, as mothers in that era were so old-fashioned.

Selecting a movie was quite time-consuming. Ruth and Rose Marie loved Westerns, while Geraldine and I preferred society pictures. A society picture was one in which the actors appeared at least once in evening clothes. There was no rating system in those days, but our mothers had their own system, and the younger girls were sure to tattle if we saw a forbidden movie. At least once, Geraldine and I sneaked away and saw an X-rated film. As with reading the scandal sheet of the *Chicago Herald* and *Examiner*, the fear of getting caught far outweighed any pleasure we got out of it.

Kiki and *Flaming Youth*, the latter starring Clara Bow, got past the maternal censors somehow. We saw Mary Pickford in *Sparrows* and *Rebecca of Sunnybrook Farm*, everything with Harold Lloyd, and some of the early Chaplins. Dorothy and Lillian Gish were favorites, as was Vilma Banky. I remember one tear-jerker (name forgotten) in which Blanche Sweet sang a song, *There's a Tear for Every Smile in Hollywood*. We saw Lon Chaney in *The Hunchback of Notre Dame* and Doug Fairbanks in *Robin Hood*. (Come to think of it, our favorite uncle, who played semi-pro baseball, took us to see that one, and when Robin ran his sword right through the wicked sheriff, tough Uncle Earl passed out cold.)

A few years later, the talkies came in, and everyone went out of the theater humming or whistling the theme song. The first talkie I saw was *The Vagabond King*. The second was *The Jazz Singer*, starring Al Jolson.

In 1924, however, movies were silent and there was a piano down in front on which a lady played appropriate music. You could tell when someone was going to die or when the U.S. Cavalry was going to rescue the brave pioneers from the Indians because the music was always about 30 seconds ahead of the action, setting the mood.

Of course, we got more than a feature film for our 10 cents. There was *Pathe's News of the World*. There were animated cartoons—*Felix the Cat* or some little character who jumped out of an inkwell—and there was the Saturday serial. We saw *The Perils of Pauline* with Pearl White. Every chapter ended with Pearl hanging over a cliff, bound and gagged across the railroad track, or in the clutches of a leering villain. No other serial was ever half as good, not even *The Telephone Girl* with Albertina Rasch or *Spanky and His Gang*.

Sometimes we even had audience participation, when words of a popular song appeared on the screen, and a little white ball bounded from syllable to syllable as the piano lady played the accompaniment. The songs were mostly the ones we all knew, like *There Are Smiles That Make You Happy*, *The Prisoner's Song*, *Let Me Call You Sweetheart*, or *A Tumbledown Shack by the Old Railroad Track*.

It must have been the following summer that we all picked strawberries for a neighbor who raised them commercially. I think the pay was 15 cents an hour. I clearly remember my check for two weeks' work, the first check I ever had—it was for $8.45. Geraldine and I used part of our wealth to go to the Rialto on a weekday (it was summer vacation), and afterward we went to the best ice-cream parlor in town and had not any mere 10-cent sundae, but a parfait with three kinds of ice cream, topping, whipped cream and Nabisco wafers. It cost 35 cents.

Wow! You don't have to tell me how a millionaire feels when he buys his first yacht. I've been there! ❖

The razor grinder stood on street corners offering to sharpen gentlemen's straight razors. The powerful iceman also roamed the streets, hauling huge chunks of ice. With his huge tongs and magical ice pick he cut off pieces to fit the square iceboxes. (The top of the box held a compartment for the ice, with a drain to run the melt-off into a pan below, and the lower section was used to store food.) The kids followed his wagon on hot summer days, catching or stealing chips of ice to suck.

Then there was the happy popcorn wagon with its small flame to heat the butter. The squeal of its steam whistle brought kids running when they could beg a nickel from Father. Mother would gladly donate the nickel and more if he carried the much coveted "sauerkraut candy" made from coconut strips and taffy.

The ragman was always a little dirty, often unshaven and dressed in a potpourri of clothes (usually a long black overcoat with a hundred pockets) he had picked from customers. (Despite his appearance, it was neighborhood gossip that he spent his winters in Florida: "Hey, Sam, tell the truth, where *do* you go in winters?" "In the barn with the horses," he would snap.) Some mothers used him as the neighborhood bogeyman, threatening their little children that he would carry them off if they didn't behave. Some tots took the admonition so much to heart that at the first faint tone of his jingle or the *clip-clop* of his horse, small bikes, homemade scooters made from orange crates and roller skates, and raggy-tailed britches disappeared into sundry yards, leaving a deserted street for the defamed rag wagon.

The strolling newspaper boy, who chose likely crossroads or corners to hawk his papers, was also a familiar sight, and many a kid envied his daring and business sense. Other youngsters, hoping to cash in on his territory, would buy a bundle at wholesale and try to emulate his technique—usually with rather disastrous results. Somehow customers knew who the genuine newsboys were and whether or not the startling news they were hollering was really important.

And then there were the Greeks and Italians with their seasonal vegetables and fruits, tomatoes in early summer, peaches in late. The banana man, with his green pushcart, handlebar mustache and red hankie, would shout, "How's about a banana?" in a voice like grand opera. And there was the watermelon wagon, with a big yellow umbrella shading the huckster.

Along the seacoast, in cities such as Baltimore and Boston, oyster vendors chanted their songs as they pushed their carts with tables attached containing plates, vinegar and condiments. There were sweet potato men, pepper pot ladies and hominy hucksters. They sold freshly ground horseradish that would barbecue your throat. Everything imaginable to eat was carried in the streets. Some even carried huge pans filled with hot cakes and gingerbread sweets, all topped with tasty flies.

There were street musicians, too. The organ grinder, the banjo and concertinas and the mouth organ virtuosos added joy to the streets.

But eventually the chain store and the quick-delivery delicatessen drove them all out of business. Actually, there had always been opposition to the street peddlers from shopkeepers who protested that much of their prospective sales went to the traveling vendors.

In very early America, peddlers sold all sorts of items on the road. Some were specialists in clocks, chairs, cotton goods, books, candles, harness goods, tinware or hardware, while others carried the whole kaboodle. They were known as trunk peddlers, for they carried their wares in a small trunk on their back and sometimes in a wagon. People then, it must be remembered, lived widely scattered around the countryside without even a general store within scores of miles, even hundreds. Even in the

> *The powerful iceman also roamed the streets, hauling huge chunks of ice. With his huge tongs and magical ice pick he cut off pieces to fit the square iceboxes.*

through. Everyone would drop what they were doing and rush to his wagon.

The peddler in early America helped open the West and push civilization farther and faster than it would have progressed without him. No sooner did a settler open up a new homestead as far west as Kentucky or Tennessee in the 1870s than a peddler would come to his door with the little trinkets—thread, needle, pencils, spoons, combs, etc.—that he desperately needed. Peddlers had just as tough a time crossing the wilderness as the first settlers, but they made it with their packs on their backs.

It might be said that early American peddlers laid the foundations of big business as we know it today. Take, for instance, the first crude handiwork of making combs. Early ones were made from wood. But one ingenious New Englander decided to make one out of horn. It worked so well that a factory had to satisfy the demand. Pins, buttons and tinware all followed suit when the demand rose from the peddlers.

sophisticated metropolis of New York in 1850, almost all kinds of household products were sold on the streets: root beer, strawberries, whale oil, oysters, bread, and even meat.

It was often to the poorer classes that the peddler offered his goods and services, and they blessed him for it. But a peddler working the back roads had to exchange his goods for farm produce and farm-made items. He turned these into cash when he got to the nearest town. Indeed, farm life would have been intolerably dull without the visit from a wandering peddler.

These early itinerant peddlers were not always of the best moral fiber, and some would be gone from the village or neighborhood once they had sold their shabby wares. But these were in the minority. Many peddlers returned time and again to the routes they had established.

Peddlers were eagerly welcomed when they visited a small village, not only for their wares, but for the gossip they brought from other neighborhoods and towns they had passed

Some of these roving merchants managed to accumulate great wealth in time. For instance, Collis Potter Huntington carried two tin boxes of hardwood, thread and combs for a spell. Later he opened a store, and later yet he became president of the Pacific and Central Pacific Railroads.

Another famous pushcart graduate was Patsy D'Agostino, who came to America in 1920, sold vegetables from a pushcart, and became a millionaire grocery chain owner and president of the National Association of Retail Grocers.

Peddlers have all but vanished from the American scene. Occasionally, a few picturesque survivors of another age are seen attracting customers, more out of nostalgia rather than necessity. They are a faint echo from a most happy period when most of us were growing up. "Rags! … Fresh popcorn! … Get your umbrella fixed ! … Scissors sharpened! … Tomatoes, potatoes! … Get a pot that never rusts!" Buy a memory that never fades. ❖

Delicious Memories

Chapter Two

Decades ago when Janice and I were courting, I liked to take her to a Saturday night picture show in town. Like so many other young folks, we always liked to stop off at the soda fountain before the show (it was always closed afterwards).

Our soda fountain was located in the local drug store—one of countless similar establishments across the country which doled out sweet ice cream sodas or soft drinks mixed right there before your thirsty eyes. There was nothing quite like sharing a soda with your best girl on a Saturday night.

Our Hometown drug store had the traditional fountain with stools (usually lined with youthful patrons) and a booth section with two or three tables. When I was young, I thought the establishment was huge. After passing the soda fountain, along one wall were displays of various merchandise—from foot powders to shaving soaps to personal items. I remember there was aspirin for sale, but not the endless displays of pain relievers like today. I guess there are a lot more headaches now than we had back then.

There was a selection of candies on the store's main aisle. You had to pass it to get back to the reading section where my favorite magazines of war and western pulp fiction were on display. There was, of course, the obligatory handwritten sign proclaiming, "Buy first, then read!" I usually couldn't afford to buy either candy or magazines if I expected to take Janice out for an ice cream soda and a movie on Saturday night.

Years later, on trip back home to visit my parents, Janice and I returned to that same drug store. It wasn't as cavernous as I remembered it. There was still a soda fountain; modernized, but still there. About 15 years ago I returned again to find it replaced by a delicatessen.

Today I miss those delicious days that filled our hometown. Those ice cream sodas are just the start of memories of a time before red meat, butterfat and high cholesterol became dirty words to nutritionists and physicians. When I was working at my first "town" job after Janice and I married, my favorite stop was at the bakery, where a "baker's dozen" donuts were waiting to accompany me many mornings to the office. On the way home it might be a stop at the butcher shop for a chop, a roast or ribs for one of Janice's scrumptious meals.

My favorite memory, however, is of taking my son to the candy counter at the old general store (the same one to which my own father had taken me in my childhood) and seeing his eyes light up with the sweet possibilities that a dime could bring.

The soda fountain, the candy counter, the butcher shop and the early grocery stores provided our hometowns every tasty necessity—or desire—we could envision. These reminiscences take us back to the days when we were eternally young, when we didn't know what calories and cholesterol were, when a trip to the grocery for Mama was a safe adventure for any youngster. It's been years since I tasted an ice cream soda. Drop by the soda fountain with Janice and me as we order up some delicious memories.

—By Ken Tate

granulated, brown and soft white. Soft white was the same texture as brown without the color. (I wonder whatever happened to it?) Each barrel had its own scoop and we weighed what the customer wanted.

Coffee was in the bean, although it came in pound packages. Every household had its own grinder. As the cook started the meal by building a fire of coal or wood in her big, black, iron range, one of the children was delegated to grind the coffee. This was then measured into a large enamel coffee pot with the right amount of water, generally a potful, and allowed to come to a boil. Then it was pushed to the back of the stove where there was less heat and the grounds were allowed to settle. Believe it or not, it was good.

I don't remember selling a pack of cigarettes. It was a "roll-your-own" era and a pack of papers was given with each bag of tobacco. If a woman had been seen smoking a cigarette, the shock waves would have reached all over the county.

Cheese came in a big wheel and was cut with a large knife. (I never could learn how to gauge it to cut the right amount; I suppose it was accomplished with lots of practice.) Unless my memory is very bad, this was the only kind we had. The large variety of cheeses in today's stores was unheard of then.

I don't remember selling a pack of cigarettes. It was a "roll-your-own" era and a pack of papers was given with each bag of tobacco. If a woman had been seen smoking a cigarette, the shock waves would have reached all over the county. There were also bags of chewing tobacco, and I am told that Mail Pouch and Red Man are still available. Some of the men preferred plug tobacco for chewing. It came in long bars and we had a cutter with graduations to tell how much to cut. Cigars came in wooden boxes and were kept in a showcase. We didn't dare pick up the cigars individually. We took the box out of the case and the customer took what he wanted. I don't know why that was a rule. We could handle crackers, but not cigars!

Dry goods consisted of the odds and ends one buys in a dime or variety store now. Yard goods consisted mainly of several patterns of calico, gingham and muslin, bleached and unbleached. Then we got ritzy and added several patterns of percale. Thread was black or white—no colors.

We sold "coal oil" by the gallon for lighting and starting fires. I can't remember calling it kerosene. Cookstoves which burned it were just beginning to come on the market. This was certainly a boon for the housewife in the summer, when she was canning fruits and vegetables for the winter. Vinegar came in barrels, too.

These are just a few of the many items that were available in a village general store. After 60 years, it is hard to remember many of them. I suppose one reason for remembering these things is that they offer such a contrast to the marketing of today.

I am glad that I have been privileged to live in today's world, as well as that of the early part of the century. Don't let anyone tell you it is getting worse! Bad things happened then, too, but we only heard about our own community much later. With more people to get into trouble and with radio and television, today we hear it all instantly. We also hear things we never would have heard about in those days, so everything *seems* worse.

Oh, I have my moments when I start wallowing in nostalgia. But all I need to do to bring me back to reality is get some crackers from their waxed-paper container and a slice of individually wrapped cheese, make myself cup of instant coffee with water quickly heated by electricity, and enjoy it. When some "old-timer" starts yapping about how much better the Good Old Days were in comparison to the present, just remember the crackers. ❖

Rainbows & Big Brothers

By Leta Fulmer

It had been a rainbow-colored day for me, one of those rare days when everything seems to go just right, even for a 5-year-old. Buster had even obeyed my commanding voice when the postman came. He'd reserved his nipping fox terrier teeth for another time, though he hungrily eyed the blue-clad legs. My speckled banty hen had flustered from the shed, clucking hysterically at her brand-new chicks. Mom had finally let me take off my winter underwear, and I stared admiringly at legs that were smooth and sleek without the wrap-around bulge of long johns.

And now, the icing on the cake! Big Brother, most of the time an abomination in his almost-grown-up superiority, had laughingly tossed me a handful of pennies. Clutching them tightly in my fist, I tricycled to the corner store.

At the door, I paused and took a long breath to boost my courage, for though the sign read Summers Grocery, it should have read Winters! Mr. Summers was a grumpy little man with a raspy, impatient voice and colorless eyes, as icy as the pop bottle he constantly turned around and around in his wrinkled hand. Only the demanding need to satisfy my sweet tooth brought me to that sagging screen door. I closed it very, very carefully, for the slightest bang of that screen was invitation to reprimands and insults!

Silently, I stood before the showcase, peering at the array of candy. Should it be gumdrops, pepperminty red or sharply wintergreen? Or maybe chocolate drops with towering peaks and chewy cream inside? Licorice whips tempted me as they angled this way and that in a tall glass. I tried to sort out my ponderings. Perhaps I should get four different things. After all, I had four pennies.

Big Brother, most of the time an abomination in his almost-grown-up superiority, had laughingly tossed me a handful of pennies.

"Well!" The sharp, cutting word made me jump, and I looked into piercing eyes that willed me to get it over and done with. "I suppose you're going to spend an hour to buy a penny's worth of candy!"

"I've got four pennies, Mr. Summers." I had to push the words past the gathering lump in my throat. "My brother—"

"I couldn't care less about your brother." He grabbed a pink-and-green sack and snapped it open. "Hope you've made up your mind."

"Well," I hesitated, "I think I want two gumdrops, one red and one green—"

"You'll take them as they come," he snapped, and dropped two white ones in the bag. "Now what?" He mumbled under his breath words I was glad I couldn't hear.

"I'll take some chocolate drops and some licorice—oh, wait a minute."

"You durned kids are enough to drive a man crazy! Don't know why I bother to stock candy. It's just an aggravation! Here!"

Far back in the case I'd spied something new: tiny paraffin bottles filled with syrup-sweet liquid, red and green and yellow. When the liquid was gone, the bottle could be chewed like gum. They were exactly what I wanted. Wanted badly enough to brave Mr. Summers' wrath. "Oh, Mr. Summers, that's what I truly want, 4 cents' worth, please!"

"You durned kids are enough to drive a man crazy! Don't know why I bother to stock candy. It's just an aggravation! Here!" He plopped the striped sack on the counter. "This is what you picked, this is what you get!"

I stared at the miniature bottles I wanted so badly. I looked at the sack and the clawlike hand outstretched for my money. Eyes brimming with frustrated tears, I slowly backed away. I even banged the door, banged it hard and on purpose. Mr. Summers' accusing voice followed me down the street.

I must have looked like a total disaster when I burst into our kitchen, nose running, tears marking a zigzag path down my dusty cheeks. I sobbed out my story in Big Brother's arms that were surprisingly gentle.

"Come on, Sis." He grinned, but his chin stuck out just like Daddy's. "Come on, we're going to the store." And away we went. I pulled back a little as we neared the store, but he pushed me in ahead of him.

Mr. Summers peered at us over the top of his glasses and fought hard to force a smile.

Big Brother did indeed look grown-up in that dinky little room. He simply towered over the

suddenly friendly Mr. Summers, who seemed to be bracing himself for an attack that never came.

Instead, my brother lingered before the counter, laconically discussing with me the merits and drawbacks of each assortment. With exaggerated indecision, he picked first one candy, then another, changing his mind as soon as it hit the sack.

Mr. Summers fidgeted and fawned, almost pitifully eager to please, forcing his creaky voice into a semblance of friendly helpfulness. Big Brother dawdled and dickered so long that even I became impatient, but Mr. Summers hung on tight to his pasted-on cheerfulness and polite manner. Finally, Big Brother turned to me with a twinkling grin.

"Hey, Sis, I think what we really want are those dinky little bottles filled with that colored stuff, don't you?" Of course, I nodded enthusiastically, and a gleam of mischief touched his eyes as he continued, "Mr. Summers, while you're at it, I think maybe we should have a different sack, don't you? That one looks kind of beat up."

Out we went, letting the screen door slam with a reverberating bang. I could hear the old man's sigh of deep relief. I almost felt a little sorry for him, but not quite.

Hand in hand, we walked down the street. It was beginning to get dark. Opening the rainbow-colored sack, I picked out the paraffin bottle and bit off the end. Slowly, so as to savor every luscious drop, I sucked out the sweet pink juice. Umm, umm, that was good! Almost as good as having a Big Brother! ❖

Hometown Celebrations

Chapter Three

The
includi
crosse:
with th
the Gr
of the
units p
We lov
route;
the cu
that ar
Af
began
festivi
firewo
ever tc
be
fill
on
the
big
to
Th
bee

tim
De
yea
roc
pri
ma
gri
to
pla
hel

par
of
egg
fro

sid
wa
cer

the
dre
fee
nee

the sa
Th
lots of
it was
missec

It is perhaps hard to imagine today, but there was a time when hometown celebrations revolved around holidays. It's equally hard to imagine, but those celebrations also brought virtually everything else in town to a standstill. It's easy to explain why.

First, there were fewer observed holidays where people actually got time off. When you did get a holiday off from work, it was truly cause for a celebration.

Besides getting off every Sunday, my father worked at the lumberyard where he was employed every day of the year other than New Year's Day, Decoration Day (now Memorial Day), Independence Day, Thanksgiving and Christmas. Others may have had other holidays, but that was all he was given. Daddy had a one-week vacation after about a decade of lumberyard employment, but he always worked through it in exchange for a check with double pay. Times were hard.

When a holiday did come around, it was a holiday for *everyone*, or so it seemed. That meant schoolmates, friends and family were all released from the rigors of reality for a sweet 24-hour period of freedom—and the whole community made the best of it.

Take Memorial Day as an example. When Janice and I were young, the celebration began as families and different veterans' groups went to every cemetery in town and throughout the county to place flags on the graves of dead patriots.

I was a Boy Scout, so I always helped with the flag placement. It taught me to take pride in this great country, and to revere those men and women who had fought and died to protect all of us and our freedom. It also imbued me with thankfulness to God for the blessings He had given us through the faithfulness of our forebears.

After the cemeteries were decorated, a parade down Main Street culminated in the center of town. (It seems that parades were much more a part of holiday celebrations back then. Most hometowns didn't need much of a reason to hold a parade.)

After the parade, folks would gather for patriotic speeches and recognition of veterans. Many of our younger generation would hardly believe it, but it doesn't seem that long ago when Civil War veterans celebrated with World War I veterans in doughboy green. Every year we all sadly watched those Blue and Gray ranks dwindle and disappear; today very few veterans of the "war to end all wars" survive.

The holiday ended with another ubiquitous part of most holidays—a concert in the bandstand on the courthouse square.

Today Memorial Day has been reduced to another reason for a three-day weekend. Some of our young folks help old-timers like me go out and decorate cemeteries, but it's not the kind of family and community holiday that it once was. With these stories let's remember a time when holidays pulled us all together in community and national pride.

How I miss those Hometown Celebrations!

—*Ken Tate*

After our curiosity was satisfied, Mrs. Colvin, with some difficulty, got the horse turned around and we headed back to town to get a vantage point from which to view the parade. The courthouse yard was our choice, for it was above street level, with grass and shade. That was the old courthouse, which was removed a few years later to make room for the present county building. Many other people gathered, and soon the grown-ups were visiting and the children were milling about.

Far off down the street, strains of band music were heard. Everyone craned his neck and moved into a more advantageous position to get first sight of the coming parade. We waited impatiently. When the band came into view, the players were perched high on a wagon, each man dressed in a natty uniform, playing catchy tunes on instruments that glittered and sparkled in the sunlight. There were other bands spaced at intervals along the 5-mile-long parade. Father down the line was the clown band, dressed their funniest and playing bent, demolished instruments, but the tunes were lively.

Circus wagons were truly works of art. They were decorated with carved figures and scroll-work. The paint was bright and new. The driver's seat was high, and he proudly braced himself as he drove several teams of beautifully matched horses. People's hearts just naturally skipped a beat or two as the bands passed.

Many of the wagons carried caged animals: haughty lions, angry bears, pacing leopards and tigers that wished there were no bars. Monkeys, of course, drew the greatest attention. Besides, there were herds of elephants, camels and zebras that walked sedately along the way.

Something that gave us all the creeps was the snake wagon. Inside the glass enclosure sat a young woman in white with an assortment of snakes draped around her neck for a necklace. The floor was covered with the wiggly, crawly creatures. We wondered how she could sit still in such a place. The very last feature was the steam calliope. The man I envied sat at a keyboard and rippled out rollicking tunes.

The crowd dispersed and our mothers rounded us up. We found our conveyance and drove a few blocks to Mineral Palace Park. Inside the park, we drove along winding drives, past colorful flower beds, by the placid Lake Clara, to a spot not far from the palace. Under

some shade trees, a big white tablecloth was spread on the grass. The baskets were opened, and the goodies began to appear.

First came a big white banana cake, with banana slices tucked away in the frosting. Then another—a chocolate cake with thick, thick icing that made one glad he was alive. That was decades before cake mixes. Then came the luscious cherry pies with their unforgettable flavor and drippy sweetness. A platter of golden fried chicken took its place in the middle of the tablecloth. The potato salad was mixed with minced onion and chopped pickles with a hint of vinegar. It was decorated with slices of hard-boiled eggs. We had not heard of mayonnaise or commercial salad dressing. The sandwiches were slices of bread, spread with real butter and

homemade jelly. Peanut butter was in the future for us. Did ever a monarch dine so well?

All gathered around the feast, sat on the grass and enjoyed the food and conversation. Presently, a horse and buggy went dashing along one of the drives.

"A runaway, a runaway," someone yelled. "Oh, Mrs. Colvin, that's your horse!" And sure enough, it was. The lunch was forgotten while several went to assess the damage. A worker in the park stopped the horse. A buggy shaft was broken so that it could not be used. The man pulled the buggy back under a portico of the palace until it could be taken home.

Some good neighbors gave us a ride home, while the horse walked behind. So ended a very special day in our lives. ❖

bearing the likeness of a sumo wrestler. Sporting a cherubic face with dimpled chin, the warrior was most impressive. One muscular arm served as a handle, the other a spout. It became a treasured conversation piece used only for special occasions, and after more than half a century, the sumo teapot is still in trim condition without a chip or crack to mar its surface.

Merchants lining the avenue of memory called Main Street offered little in the way of holiday decorations to dazzle the eye at Christmastime. Just a swag of glitter to outline the curve of a store front, a touch of fresh holly, perhaps a gaily lit tree or two—these were frugal times.

The first inkling that Christmas was beginning to weave its magic was the arrival of a package from our maiden aunt, Annie. The package always contained a new sweater for each of us.

The closer it came to the holidays, the sweeter our house became. Mom insisted she was a plain cook, but we knew better. Her fruitcake was guaranteed to turn any fruitcake-hater into a true believer.

Tree trimming was a job reserved for the younger generation. We quickly tired of draping strands of tinsel in a perfect parade over each branch and instead wadded the strands into small balls and let them fall where they would. Ever the perfectionist, our big sister sneaked back into the living room during the dead of night and redid the tree to her own liking.

Christmas triggers flashbacks to the child in all of us, spiced with the tenderness and longing of all our yesterdays. My grandchild, eyes brimming with wonder, asks me, "What was Christmas like in the old days, Grandma?" I wince and look around to ask someone of the older generation and then realize I'm it! I try my best to explain to her that Christmas never changes and is neither old nor new. Christmas is love. May yours be a joyful one. ❖

The Week After Christmas

By Mrs. O.C. Ulrich

The week before Christmas was a wonderful time in our town, even if the Depression was just getting started. But it was the week after Christmas that was a high point in our winter school holiday. The merchants were getting ready for us to make our begging rounds.

Xenia, Ohio, was exactly the right size town for our purpose—not too large to cover in a couple of days and not too small to make our load of loot skimpy.

We were the public relations team for the town businessmen. They ordered little gifts that carried their advertising, and we were the means of distributing the stuff to the households of Xenia. They were happy to get the stuff out, and we were happy to be their legmen.

Bundled in our heavy coats, mufflers, mittens and galoshes, we waded through the snowy streets on our mission, asking everywhere and always politely, "Are you giving out any free stuff?"

Mabel, Irma, Miriam and I were one of the teams of four that made the calls. Merchants seemed to be a bit cross if more than four of us arrived for the New Year's Eve "trick or treat."

Mabel came down from Orient Hill; Irma came across the street from her father's grocery store; and we all left from our big brick house on South Detroit Street. Past the big shoe factory and the viaduct, we trudged to the combination coal and ice company, which would deal out ice picks. Then it was on to the lumberyard, which gave us rulers, yardsticks or maybe a big calendar that was almost as fancy

Merchants seemed to be a bit cross if more than four of us arrived for the New Year's Eve "trick or treat."

as a valentine, with pictures of pretty ladies and pockets to hold grocery notes.

We got pen wipers, penholders and pencils in various office and stores. The insurance men gave us blotters.

Shoup's Grocery Store handed out shopping bags, which came in handy because our school book bags wouldn't hold all the gifts. Mr. Shoup often passed each one of us a little green pickle that read "Heinz 57 varieties," which we wore on ribbons around our necks.

The department store (I think it was a Boston Store) was a veritable treasury. In the toy department, we were sometimes given puzzles; in the stationery department, we got covers to protect our schoolbooks; and in the cosmetics department, the lady gave us cuticle boards.

The drugstore saved up its annual supply of Tangee lipsticks (the only kind we were permitted to use) to give to the girl beggars.

The climax of the tour would be Geyer's Book Store, which had a little section for eating. They would give us fancy bookmarks and serve us a bowl of hot soup for a nickel (with plenty of crackers) and a giant slice of pumpkin pie for another nickel.

If our parents or grandparents were generous enough, we had about a half-pint of whipped cream (the real stuff) on the pie for another nickel.

We felt fine and warm and full as we walked the mile home, bearing our gifts like trophies to lay down before our admiring families.

Christmas gifts came all week in Xenia, Ohio, in the year 1927! ❖

Chautauqua's Coming!

By Paul Long

Back at the turn of the century and into the early '30s, this announcement brought jubilation to citizens, young and old, across North America and especially to the small, rural towns far from the entertainment of larger cities. Before talking movies and access to radio programming, the coming of the Chautauqua tents was the next best thing to having the circus come to town.

The Chautauqua likely evolved from the old lyceum movement, which dates back to 1826. The purpose of the lyceum was to present programs to promote self-culture and community instruction. Thoreau, Lowell, Greeley, Emerson and Beecher lectured from the lyceum stage. Utilizing aspects of the lyceum, the Chautauqua assembly was developed in 1874 at Chautauqua, N.Y., for the study of the Bible and Sunday school methods. The idea spread across America and gradually the programs were expanded. Soon, Chautauqua companies presented a hybrid program composed of religious training, education, culture and entertainment.

Few today have heard of Chautauqua or know the excitement and romance these touring performers brought to town.

While most of the Chautauquas were presented in canvas tents, a few early ones were given in permanent buildings known as assemblies. One of the strongest and earliest assemblies in the prairie states was the Chautauqua in Ottawa, Kan. The Ottawa Assembly was a thriving offspring of Mother Chautauqua in New York, developed in 1883 under the leadership of clergyman Duncan Milner. With the support of the citizenry of Ottawa, a huge auditorium was built, and the local assembly brought some notables to the little Midwestern city.

Traveling Chautauquas were of two kinds—those artists sent out on a circuit by a Chautauqua bureau and Chautauquas presented with talent contracted by a local committee. Most of the Chautauquas were of the former. The popularity of the Chautauqua is realized when it is noted that slightly after the turn of the century, some 10,000 communities were circuit towns.

In addition to the artists who presented the programs, numerous personnel were necessary for the Chautauqua: a platform super-intendent, a crew foreman, several crew or tent boys and a junior director (always a young lady). The crew foreman directed the crew

EPWORTH PARK

THE GREEN SPOT

UNDER THE OLD OAKS

EPWORTH PARK CHAUTAUQUA ASSEMBLY
BETHESDA, OHIO

JULY 22nd TO AUGUST 5th 1922

THIRTY-SECOND SEASON

America. Some of these were the White & Meyers Chautauqua System, Ben Franklin's Cadmean Westcoast Fives Circuit, the Redpath-Horner Premier Circuit and the Lyric Chautauquas. With headquarters in Kansas City, Mo., the Redpath-Horner organization was one of the most influential in the Midwest.

One enterprising bureau manager worked out an ingenious system for moving the troupes and equipment from town to town on a circuit without suffering "open dates" and wasting a day in moving. Other companies quickly adopted this strategy. Simply, the given circuit had at least one more performance tent and troupe than the number of days of a circuit. Thus, a six-day circuit would have seven tents with seven troupes of performers.

For example, with a six-day circuit performing in six towns, on day one, tent No. 1 was set up in town one. On day 2, tent No. 2 was set up in town 2, and so on, until on day 6, Chautauqua performances were going on in the six circuit towns. Tent No. 7, meanwhile, was moving to a new circuit town. On day 7, tent No. 7 was up in town No. 1 of the new circuit and performing, so tent No. 1 would leap-frog and move on to town No. 2 of the new circuit.

What were the programs like?

Even today, after nearly six or seven decades have passed, much of the program material presented still looks interesting. Such notable Americans as Booker T. Washington, William Jennings Bryan, Gifford Pinchot, Clarence Darrow, Robert N. Follette, former president Rutherford B. Hayes and future presidents William McKinley and Howard Taft spoke from the Chautauqua stages.

Programs included religious presentations, travel lectures with stereopticon views and many varieties of musical performance, such as bands, quartets, mezzo-sopranos, pianists and bagpipe bands.

boys in their tasks of erecting the tents, setting up the stage and seating facilities, selling and collecting tickets, ushering and assisting the junior director in teaching and entertaining the youngsters of the communities. In much the manner of the circus, the bureaus also sent out advance men, or campaign directors. They arrived in town several days ahead of the scheduled Chautauqua troupe and created excitement with intensive advertising and advance ticket sales.

During the heyday of Chautauqua, a number of companies, or bureaus, provided touring circuits, which brought the performances to rural

During the decades of Chautauqua popularity, automobiles were scarce and roads were often impassable. For this reason, many Chautauqua patrons traveled by railroad to the city where the performance was being held. Most towns had passenger service with trains arriving and departing the local Chautauquas and advertised "reduced fares on all railroads" during Chautauqua days.

Farm families often came to town during Chautauqua week and remained throughout the programs. This was mainly due to the poor transportation conditions, but also because the days of the Chautauqua were a time of socializing and vacationing for hardworking, entertainment-hungry rural residents. Local committees erected tents in the vicinity of the big Chautauqua tent in which patrons could sleep and cook their meals. Advertising for the Chautauqua in one Midwest city noted that "the grounds are in town, and tents have all conveniences of water, lights, etc." Reportedly, some 400 tents were erected.

By the latter part of the '20s, enthusiasm for Chautauquas waned, and many tents were folded for the last time. The advent of the talking movie, the development of theaters with air conditioning and the accessibility to radio brought a demand for different and more sophisticated forms of entertainment.

In a few years, those wonderful interludes of excitement and entertainment were forever gone. Only memories remain of those far-off times when the harvest was done and the corn laid by, and city folks and farm folks could spend a few days away from the drabness of everyday life. Little wonder they thrilled to the words "Chautauqua's coming!" ❖

attack, hanging on the sides of their horses, firing over their horses' backs. We could scarcely see the Indians at all, maybe a few feathers sticking up over the animal's neck. One of the mysteries of the act to me was how the Indians and white men could fall from their horses in a dead run, pretending they had been shot, and not get hurt, which they evidently could do, since they put on the same act day after day.

In the next act, Buffalo Bill gave a demonstration of his marvelous marksmanship with a rifle. He and another rider would come riding into the ring as fast as their horses could run. The other rider would toss glass or clay balls into the air, and Buffalo Bill would invariably break them before they reached the ground. Next, the rider tossed up two and even three balls at a time, and still none of them ever reached the ground before Buffalo had broken them. This might explain how Cody had so many scrapes with the Indians and still kept his scalp.

It was the last act that really rang the bell for us boys. I would not know what to call it, other than a review of the nations. Instead of the soldiers marching, they came riding into the ring at top speed, each man carrying a flag of his particular nation. The flags were on staffs some 8 or 10 feet long, so the flags were well above the heads of the riders. They were in squads of 8 or 10, and instead of riding around the ring and taking up a position, they just continued riding. Every minute or two, a new group would enter riding, until there were at least 100 men riding pell-mell around the ring.

The amazing thing was that about half of them seemed to be riding in one direction and the other half in the other direction. How they could do that and not collide was what puzzled us boys. What seemed to be utter bedlam and confusion was in reality an exhibition of skillful riding and horse-manship at its finest.

There was loud cheering when men representing different nations came into the ring; this was especially true when the German soldiers appeared. But you should have heard the deafening roar that went up when a dozen boys came in wearing U.S. Cavalry uniforms and carrying the Stars and Stripes. We boys stood up on our seats and yelled just as loud as the rest of them.

Darkness had fallen over the countryside long before we reached home that night. We were tired, but happy, boys, and when, at last, sleep came, in our dreams Buffalo Bill and the Indians just kept on riding.

All in all, it was a wonderful, thrill-packed, never-to-be-forgotten day. ❖

One of the mysteries of the act to me was how the Indians and white men could fall from their horses in a dead run, pretending they had been shot, and not get hurt.

Trolley Parties

By Mrs. Lewis Matzek

Those of us who grew up in Denver, Colo., will remember those hilarious trolley rides way back in 1908 or 1909. Some of us small-fry, a bit too young to participate, could only sit on the curb and enviously watch this gaiety go by, but we could hope that such merriment would be the "in" thing when we grew up.

The special open-air cars, tramway equipment, had seats like benches extending from side to side, with steps resembling running boards along the outside. Here the more daring young swains liked to stand. Here, too, they could be more fully admired for their sartorial splendor—candy-striped silk shirts, ice-cream pants, sailor-type straw hats and white shoes.

The girls, wearing frothy summer dresses, occupied the seats, competing for the end seats.

Strings of gaily colored lights outlined the roof of the car.

In this crowd there were sure to be a banjo and a couple of mandolins, as well as numerous young voices happily raised in the songs of that day.

As the tramway crisscrossed the city, these excursions toured many new and unfamiliar districts. Trolley rides were sponsored by churches, lodges, schools, perhaps even individuals who chose this unique way to entertain friends.

Of course, all this laughter and fun could be heard for blocks. Then the cry would go up, "Here comes a trolley party!" How quickly we left our fenced yards to scamper for the street. By way of joining up, we might toss flowers or call jokes.

As all this joy faded into the distance, we morosely returned to our own games, not realizing that by the time we reached that longed-for age, trolley rides would be long gone, replaced by coonskin coats, rumble seats and the Charleston. ❖

sometimes young couples slipped away to steal a few kisses in the back seats of these.

The practice at that time was to hold a shivaree for newly married couples. This consisted of a group of people gathering around the house of the bride and groom and making a great deal of noise until the man would come outside and pass around drinks. The group would then allow the couple to continue their night in peace.

Though the custom was usually only observed for those marrying the first time, a group of townspeople decided to do a shivaree for a widower who had remarried. The groom was stubborn and refused to either come outside or provide drinks.

The result was utter confusion. The crowd used bells, washtubs and anything that would make noise. They even used some big saws from the mill, setting them up on the porch. They kept the racket going for two days. A man coming in on the train from a nearby town refused to get off. He went on to the next stop instead.

Still, that stubborn, old tightwad wouldn't come out until finally somebody turned in a fire alarm. When the horses and fire wagon came out, the groom finally gave them their drinks and everybody left.

This was before the time of radios, and phonographs were few, but Orange, like most other small towns, had a guard company, and every company had its band. The band was a big institution, and the Orange group played with the Houston Light Guards all over the state. At the dedication of the new capitol building at Austin, Phillip Sousa led the Texas bands, including the Orange group.

The whole town enjoyed the sport of baseball—from the back-lot games for the kids to the big contest between the men's teams in each town. This was an all-weather sport—rain or shine, you played ball, and for some, the muddier the field, the better!

Orange also boasted an opera house, which attracted many of the big singing stars of the day, as well as fine orchestras. Local bands also provided entertainment there. The movie houses hired piano players to provide music for the silent pictures and during intermissions.

Home dances were the vogue, and elaborate masquerade balls, as well as formal affairs, were staged at the homes of some of the wealthier residents. Bands were hired for those dances, which often lasted all night long.

The old opera house stood on the corner of Sixth and Division and played a prominent part in the town's social life. It was said to have the largest stage of any opera house in the area.

Perhaps the single highlight of the year for everybody was the big parade.

Every possible contrivance was used to offer something unique or different. Once, a leading citizen donned the dress of a woman and was locked in a cage with a live snake (harmless, of course).

Those were some of the good old days in my hometown—how I wish they could return! ❖

The Best Things in Life Are Won

By Calla Petersen

In those days it was the custom for stores to have a yearly contest in which a valuable prize was given to the winner. These prizes were sometimes diamond rings, gold watches or furs. Bert Chase, owner of Chase's Store, decided to give away a piano in 1913.

It was quite a project. First the piano had to be purchased and taken to the store for display. Then the ballots had to be printed—perhaps a thousand of them. Lastly an announcement had to be printed in the local newspaper. The customer who used a ballot was assured of quality merchandise and was allowed one vote for each dollar spent.

None of the prizes offered had ever tempted my 14-year-old sister, Jennie, but at the announcement of a piano as a prize, she was ecstatic.

It was the custom for stores to have a yearly contest in which a valuable prize was given to the winner. These prizes were sometimes diamond rings, gold watches or furs.

"Oh, Mama," she trilled, "can I enter the contest? Can I try to win the piano? May I?"

"You will have to ask Father. It means several weeks of hard work. And how about school? Would there be time for both?"

Father asked the same questions when she approached him. "You think you could win a piano? It will mean a lot of work. And Mama needs your help here in the house. You are her oldest daughter, you know."

"That's just it," she replied. "I'm the oldest. And there are five of us to play on the piano. It seems that it is my job to win that piano for all my sisters to play."

"I'll go to Mr. Chase and find out who else has entered. Most of them will probably be older than you."

Papa came back from his talk with Mr. Chase with more confidence. The merchant liked the idea of five little sisters going door-to-door, promoting his store throughout the town. And if we won, there would be the added favorable publicity of having a piano go into a home where five sisters were waiting to learn to play it.

So Jennie became a contestant. She went to the store and was given 100 ballots with a promise of more when those were gone. At home, she wrote her name on 25 of them and began planning her campaign.

There was no working on the contest on Mondays because that was wash day, Mama's hardest day of the week. By the time school was out at 4 p.m., Mama was tired and needed some rest. It had been Jennie's practice to come home from school and take over the supper preparations while she assigned to us the care of the younger children and other Monday-night supper tasks. After supper, we spent the evening studying, for there was to be no neglect of schoolwork.

But on Tuesday, we were all to come directly home from school, then go out as a group to work on the contest. Jennie would go up one street, knocking on each door. When it opened, she would tell about the contest and how she hoped to win the prize. Two by two the others were to take another street on both sides. Sometimes we went together as Mr. Chase had suggested.

The ballots were presented as each lady was told that if she made her purchase at Chase's Store, she was sure of good merchandise and would have the opportunity to vote for Jennie.

Jennie, always polite, would introduce her sisters and explain how she hoped to win the piano so that she and her sisters would have the opportunity to play it.

The following day the piano was loaded into a dray wagon by six stout men. They gave the neighbors time enough to gather in our yard so there were plenty of onlookers when the wagon drew up and the piano was carried through our front door.

It was spring, and the days were getting longer. There were two hours of daylight after school when we could work on the contest. Up one street, then another, we distributed the ballots, the first hundred, then the second hundred, then another.

Were they being turned in at the store? We wanted to know but dared not ask. We did learn that some of the other contestants had withdrawn when they learned of the earnest energy with which the Cole sisters were working. This continued for five weeks, and in that time we covered the whole town.

At last, it was over. The final day came. The ballots were being counted in secret. At a certain hour the results would be announced.

We gathered in silent anticipation. Pappy waited with us. The winner was—Jennie Cole! Her ballots numbered almost three times those of the other competitors. There were congratulations and cries of, "Speech! Speech!"

The following day the piano was loaded into a dray wagon by six stout men. They gave the neighbors time enough to gather in our yard so there were plenty of onlookers when the wagon drew up and the piano was unloaded and carried through our front door.

Then, to everyone's surprise, Mother sat down and played melodiously, with work-scarred hands, *Home Sweet Home*. And Papa, looking around slyly lest anyone was watching, stooped and kissed his wife. ❖

Homecoming Week in a Small Town

By Virginia Hearn Machir

As a teenager in the 1930s, I remember homecoming week in the small Missouri town where I lived. I looked forward to this gala event with the anticipated enjoyment of good fellowship and fun-filled days and nights.

Our first knowledge of the coming event was when a man from the Mound City shows came to town and put up posters on every available flat surface. The sides of barns, sheds and business buildings were plastered with ballyhoo posters of dancing ladies in beautiful costumes, dogs, monkeys and a Ferris wheel, announcing the homecoming week: three big days—Aug. 12, 13 and 14, Thursday, Friday and Saturday.

The homecoming took place in the city park, which was a neat, green, grassy plot, a block square, on the north side of Main Street. In the park were a small bandstand, a drinking fountain, half a dozen wooden benches and as many huge maple shade trees.

Our first knowledge of the coming event was when a man came to town and put up posters on every available flat surface.

The Mound City shows usually arrived in town late Wednesday afternoon with their big trucks to begin setting up their equipment. When we got off from work at the local glove factory, my best friend, Edna, and I, would stroll down Main Street past the city park to watch the show get set up. The excitement of watching the workers unload the trucks and put together the brightly painted red-and-yellow Ferris wheel, merry-go-round and whip; seeing the crew erect the huge tents, while two darkly suntanned, bulging-muscled men, bare to the waist, pounded the tent stakes; and watching the monkeys in cages left Edna and me in a state of ecstasy. Only a teen-ager who has lived during this era can begin to measure the joy of those homecoming days.

Thursday afternoon was the beginning of the big event, and Main Street was roped off, blocking traffic to automobiles. People milled about on the sidewalks, in the restaurants and in the park. There was no charge to enter the grounds; therefore, people from the surrounding counties, towns and farms came. Citizens who had grown up in our town and moved away years ago arranged their vacations to coincide with homecoming week. They came from California, New York, North Dakota, Texas and almost every state. They knew they would see most of their old classmates, friends, neighbors and relatives there.

Our country village became a beehive of activity, hustle and bustle, as hundreds of automobiles roared into town over the gravel roads, stirring up clouds of dust that hung in the air over town the entire three days of the homecoming. Since there were no parking lots in those days, cars were parallel parked, bumper to bumper, on every side street leading to Main Street for blocks away. If one of your out-of-town relatives came, he might even park on your lawn, saying he couldn't find another spot near enough to the homecoming.

The sidewalks were jammed with people hurrying to and from their parked cars, and the music from the carousel could be heard any place on Main Street.

When darkness came, the many bright lights of the merry-go-round, Ferris wheel and whip added to the hoopla and carnival atmosphere.

The restaurants on Main Street did a booming business in soft drinks, sandwiches and ice cream. Many families packed picnic lunches and could be seen eating, with the hoods and trunks of their automobiles serving as tables.

Every teen-age girl in our crowd planned to have a date and a new dress for each night of the homecoming. To be without either was a catastrophe, and to be without both—well, you might as well be dead! By hook or crook, Edna and I usually managed to have new dresses and the dates.

With our dates, Edna and I would propel our way through the jam of people, hoping that all of our friends would see us, especially when they took us for a ride on the Ferris wheel, the whip and, yes, the merry-go-round. There was always the chance the Ferris wheel might stop with your seat at the top, and your date would steal a kiss. When you rode the whip and went

around a fast curve, sliding against your date, it was customary for him to put his arm around you.

It was considered risqué for your date to take you to the dancing girl show. It was whispered that some of the dancers were rather scantily dressed. When our dates asked us if we wanted to see the dancing girl show, we would giggle and say, "No." They took us to see the dog and monkey show, pitched pennies into dishes and won us big black-and-white stuffed pandas, and bought us popcorn, Cokes and ice cream cones.

Little boys and girls with cotton candy rushed helter-skelter through the crowds. Adolescent boys and girls on their first dates walked around holding hands and grinned with embarrassment when we spoke to them. Parents gathered in clusters near the merry-go-round and waited for their offspring to finish their rides. The town marshal, with his silver star on the front of his shirt, was seen leading a drunk off the grounds, probably to be locked up overnight in the little rock jail on Second Street.

Relatives, friends and classmates gathered in groups and stood talking, catching up on news and gossip of the past year. The spieler from the sideshow where the dancing ladies performed could be heard going into his act: "Hurry, hurry, hurry-ee! Get your tickets now! The big show is about to begin!" Meanwhile, the dancers in their scanty costumes did bumps and grinds on the platform beside him.

In the center of the park was the huge bingo tent, which had sides that rolled up, counters made of boards around the edges for players to keep their cards on and wooden benches for seats. Here, you could sit and play bingo all afternoon and night, if you so desired, for 10 cents a game and win such gorgeous prizes as chalk Kewpie dolls, chalk collie dogs, Indian blankets, bedspreads and carnival and Depression glassware—only then they were just called glass dishes.

All during homecoming week, you could hear the caller at the bingo stand, calling out in a singsong voice over the loudspeaker, "Under N, 20-a-five, under O, six-a-teen."

There was a popcorn wagon where you could buy a sack of hot, buttered popcorn for 10 cents and a fish stand at the back of the park where you could buy a catfish sandwich for 25 cents. A merry clown with a huge bouquet of big red, yellow and blue balloons bounced around through the crowd, tempting the small-

fry with his wares. The "pop" of the rifles in the stand with the line of moving wooden ducks could be heard now and then.

The bright lights of the Ferris wheel, the music from the merry-go-round, the roar of the whip, the voice of the bingo caller, the smells of the hot, buttered popcorn and frying fish, and the hurrah and jam of people blended into a symphony called homecoming.

Now that I count my homecomings by the dozens, I still feel a quickening of my pulse when I hear the music of a carousel and see the bright lights of a Ferris wheel, no doubt stirred by the memories of teen-age homecomings in a small Missouri town.

This story would not be complete if I didn't tell you how our city park looked on Sunday morning after the homecoming when Edna and I walked by on our way to church. The pretty green grass was gone. Where the bingo stand had stood was a big dusty bare spot; where the merry-go-round had played its merry tunes was another circle of dust, and where the Ferris wheel had made its circuit in the sky was a place where the grass no longer grew. Over all were scatted popcorn sacks, popcorn, paper cups and empty soda bottles. Here and there were some pink feathers from a chalk Kewpie. Big boys and little boys walked slowly over the park with their heads down, searching for coins dropped by the ticket takers and the customers. One glance at the park, and Edna and I knew that homecoming week had come and gone. ❖

WE'RE GOING BACK TO BUFFALO

SEPT. 1ST–7TH, '07   OLD HOME WEEK   BUFFALO, N.Y.

Neighbors at Work

Chapter Four

A few years back Janice and I went to the great state of Oregon on a business trip. We were there almost a week, so we opted to rent a car to get around Portland. While there, we took a side trip to Mount Hood and stopped outside town for gasoline.

As I pulled into a small gas station, we were shocked to find an attendant and full service at the pumps. It made me think back to the days of my first real job when I was an attendant and grease monkey at a small service station in my Hometown.

It was the summer before my senior year in high school, and I had finally put together enough money to buy my first car. With that freedom in hand, I took a job at one of the stations in town. An older gentleman, Rufus by name, and I took turns manning the station along with the owner. With three of us kiiping the station open about 14 hours a day, we pumped gas and did light service work on cars in a small two-bay garage.

You learn a lot working the pumps at a small-town gas station. Diplomacy was one of the first characteristics I picked up from Carl, the owner.

"Now, Mrs. Johnson is a regular," he told me soon after I started work. "She comes in every time she starts her car, whether she needs gas or not. She'll want you to check the oil, battery and tires. When you wash the windshield, wash *all* the windows and wipe her headlamps, too. She'll be watching, so don't miss anything. Every couple of weeks or so she'll fill up with gas—she really gets persnickety then. But she's a regular, so keep her happy."

I quickly learned the idiosyncrasies of neighbors I had known for years. There was the tailor who only wanted Rufus to serve him. After all, what could some 17-year-old kid know about cars? There was the banker who watched closely to note whether I remembered to give him the little discount Carl offered to local regular customers. And there was always Mrs. Johnson.

My work at the station was a boon for high school classmates who now had a place to "hang out." Most would only buy a Nehi or a Coke and sit, talk and watch me work. Those who did buy gas usually could afford only a quarter's worth of fuel. (Guilty of the same many times, I quickly came to sympathize with attendants who had to go through the same rigmarole of service—oil, tires, windshield—for that paltry sale. To this day I hate to buy gasoline and not fill the tank.)

Daddy had taught me early to work and work hard. I learned it from his words and his example in the fields, barn lots and gardens that fed us. I learned it by helping his some summer days at the lumber mill and yard where he worked. Still, I think my first true foray off the farm and into the workaday world was what really initiated me. It was the job at that little service station that allowed me to put into practice all that Daddy had taught me—not about cars, but about honesty, character and hard work, no matter what the job.

My work there allowed me to start finding my place in the adult world of responsibility and commitment. Watching and working helped me understand what made my Hometown "tick." These stories recall those jobs, small and great, that helped pull us out of the Great Depression and put us back on our feet again. Grab your lunch and let's join our Neighbors at Work.

—Ken Tate

Shoeshine Man

By Catherine Rowell

When I was growing up in Philadelphia, any number of shoeshine men hovered in the shade of large office buildings, their shoeshine stands looking like shadows in the sun. I had gone with my dad to the barber's where he'd had a haircut. The shop smelled like bay rum so it wasn't too bad, even if it was noisy.

I knew the next stop on busy Market Street would be the shoeshine man. I liked that. I always felt sorry for the men, but my dad preferred sitting down in the cool shade.

"Shoeshine, shoeshine!" they called. "Ten cents!"

It was worth 15 cents to my dad just to relax. I watched as he eased his Lincolnesque frame into the elevated cracked-leather chair.

There was always a smile and a pleasant greeting. I watched as the shoeshine man popped open just the right shade of matching red-brown wax. How sweet it smelled! He draped his flannel cloth over the empty iron footstand and swirled the wax into my dad's good leather shoes.

It was worth 15 cents to my dad just to relax. I watched as he eased his Lincolnesque frame into the elevated cracked-leather chair.

I watched, fascinated, as he rubbed and rubbed it into the leather, almost frenzied in spite of the hot day. Not until he was entirely satisfied did he apply his magical rag. He scratched his curly white hair and made that rag sing as he popped it expertly back and forth.

I used to pretend it was one of my favorite songs, but it was probably some old-time rhythm from his own childhood. It went fast, then faster, like some gypsy melody. He popped that rag so hard and fast, he was saying, "There you are, Boss, good as new," before I came out of my trance.

I guess there was a tip. I know there was always a grin and a big "Thank you."

Soon, we were ambling down that wide street. I knew Dad looked mighty special. I also knew we were headed for a large dish of Philadelphia ice cream. I'd have … let me see … chocolate.

The shoeshine man probably has been replaced by a machine, but what machine can play your favorite tune and shine your shoes bright as a summer's day? ❖

The Organ Grinder

By Harriet E. Gowey

Among the chief delights of my early childhood, when I was growing up in a small Pennsylvania town, were the visits of the organ grinder.

In anticipation of these outstanding events, I kept a small handleless cup behind the folded back shutters on the dining room windowsill. Into this cup I regularly dropped all the pennies that came my way, in order to have them handy when I heard the organ grinder's organ as he came up our street.

The grinder was an Italian, a musical gentleman possessed of a swarthy complexion and a ready smile for all contributing children. He was quick to distinguish between youngsters who were content to stand on the fringes of the juvenile crowd and merely watch the monkey's antics and those who stepped boldly forward to positions where they could pass the lively little creature such pennies as they clutched in small, hot hands.

He doffed his tiny red cap only to youngsters who passed him genuine pennies or a rare occasional nickel.

The monkey was also a creature of great discernment. He doffed his tiny red cap only to youngsters who passed him genuine pennies or a rare occasional nickel, never to those who tried to play tricks by offering coat buttons or wooden disks.

His dances were comical. To favorite Italian tunes ground out by the wheezy little organ, he would cavort in the liveliest fashion, occasionally spinning and leaping into the air in an ecstasy of monkey energy. But on the day of which I write, the poor little creature had no energy to give his usual performance.

It was a very hot day, for one thing, and quite late in the afternoon. No matter how his master coaxed, or how energetically he ground out the strains of *Dear Napoli* or the *Carnival of Venice*, the little monkey refused to dance.

Finally, the organ grinder came to my mother. "Madam," he begged, with a courtly sweep of his well-worn cap, "my monkey is so tired that he had no heart to dance for the children. Would you permit him to take a short nap in your garden?"

"Why, certainly," my mother replied. "Pick any spot you choose and the monkey will not be disturbed there."

Soon the exhausted little creature was curled up on the cool grass in the shade of one of our rosebushes. I was entranced watching him, his tiny red cap and jacket beside him on the grass. All the lines in his wizened little face smoothed out as he lay peacefully dreaming. It was wonderful indeed!

Missing the strains of the familiar music, the other children soon came to inquire, "What has happened to the monkey?"

When I showed them our guest, asleep on the grass, they were as impressed as I, and lingered to watch his peaceful slumber with awestruck faces. What a marvelous thing to have a real live monkey condescend to take a nap in one's very own garden!

Charles Berger©

The grinder, too, lay down on the lawn and closed his eyes to the burning sky. Finally sitting up, he produced a large, newspaper-wrapped sandwich and a couple of bananas.

The monkey joined him for a late lunch. I watched entranced as the pair sat cross-legged on the grass, munching contentedly. My mother appeared with a glass of lemonade, and the monkey took a sip of that, too.

Dear, vanished childhood days, what simple pleasures brightened your enchanted hours. There were no television serials made especially for children, no Walt Disney or Sesame Street characters to fire our imaginations; only such games as we invented ourselves. But our days were rich and delightful nevertheless, and we loved our organ grinders. ❖

Songs for Sale

By R.C. McIntyre

Crowds gathered around the piano at the local five-and-dime where a clerk played and sang their favorite songs.

Originally, they were called "10-cent stores" or "five-and-dimes." The idea, originated by F.W. Woolworth, was to persuade manufacturers of soap, toothpaste and powder, shaving cream, mouthwash, perfume, cold cream, and almost any personal item to make small versions of their regular products, which would retail for 5 or 10 cents. Companies found that they made a few cents' profit from each miniature version and increased sales of their regular-size products.

Before radio became available in the late 1920s, popular songs in sheet-music form were much in demand.

During the Depression of the 1930s, customers appreciated the small products when a dime was the only money available.

Ten-cent stores eventually offered more than personal items. Toys were added, as well as greeting cards and candy. Some added a counter-and-stools restaurant with reasonably priced meals.

A well-patronized section was the sheet-music counter. Before radio became available in the late 1920s, popular songs in sheet-music form were much in demand.

If a household didn't have a phonograph to play records, the occupants had to leave home and seek entertainment at the silent movies, vaudeville, plays, company theaters or dance halls. But during the Depression, the lack of money caused many families to stay home and amuse themselves. Fortunately, almost every home had a piano, and almost every family had someone who could play it.

To boost sales of sheet music, 10-cent stores hired girls who could sing or play the piano—or both—as sheet-music clerks. Some stores hired a piano player to accompany a singing clerk. An upright piano was always found at one end of the sheet-music counter.

As the singing clerk came to the end of one song, a customer would hand her another from the array of sheet music on the counter. After repetitions of a song, she would only sing the chorus. That was the part most people wanted to hear.

Some of the 1920s–1930s hits were *Melancholy Baby, Why Do You Do Me Like You Do, Do, Do?, The Prisoner's Song, I Found a Million-Dollar Baby in a Five-and-Ten-Cent Store* and *Is Everybody Happy?*

The clerk would sing, holding the sheet music in one hand, and taking the money, ringing up the amount on the cash register, slipping the choice into a brown paper sack or rolling it and putting a rubber band around it with the other.

The free entertainment made the sheet-music counter a gathering place for people, including many high-school teens.

When talking motion pictures came into existence, the sale of sheet music became much less profitable. The counter and sheet music remained, but the pianist and singing clerk were no longer hired. ❖

Dad's Clothing Store

By Robert H. Marriott

When Dad donned his one good blue serge suit and walked the dusty 2 miles from his father's farm to the A.I. Glick clothing emporium, it may not have been the best thing that ever happened to him, but it certainly was for A.I. Glick.

I never knew what prompted that cultured gentleman with a built-in business antenna to leave the big city and open the largest retail establishment in our town of 2,000—probably the knowledge that the nearest city of any size was 16 miles distant, and that in those horse-and-buggy days, his store would attract enough prosperous farmers to keep his cash register clicking. This was before Henry invented the Model-T and provided the wheels that carried these same farmers to larger cities, spelling doomsday for the small-town merchant.

Mr. Glick had a computer mind, and when it came to facing a city-slicker suit salesman, he was a match for the best Hart-Schaffner & Marx man who ever opened a briefcase. But, being city-born-and-oriented, he had little rapport with the farmer customers who sweated it out in the wheat fields all week long, then took hurried baths, hitched Dobbin to the wagon, and took out for town and their Saturday-night outing.

It was serious business as they debated how much of the income from the haymow, corncrib or dairy cattle could be allotted to clothing the family.

Typically, Mom and Pop dispatched the younger kids to the ice-cream parlor. The teen-age girls paraded endlessly around the town square, ogled by young swains too bashful to join them, while Dad and Mom made the rounds of the stores. It was serious business as they debated how much of the income from the haymow, corncrib or dairy cattle could be allotted to clothing the family.

The day Dad walked in, Mr. Glick hit the jackpot. Dad was a darkly handsome young man, not quite 6 feet, but ramrod straight, so he looked taller. His black hair was naturally wavy, rain or shine, and unlike Mr. Glick, he could speak the special syntax of the farmer. They wanted to gab about the prospects for wheat prices, the latest in crop rotation, and would those cloud wisps in the west build up to the soaking rain the parched soil so badly needed?

Dad was a patient and sympathetic listener. His eyes mirrored their failures and their fortunes. When the preliminary small talk was over, he could have sold them most anything, but he honestly wanted to sell them only the best. A sartorial specialist, on his back a moderately priced suit looked expensive. He would make a frayed suit look wearable. Mother used to say he was the only man alive so fussy he had to have a freshly laundered shirt to go squirrel hunting. When he showed a customer a suit, it was done so dramatically you could hear bells ringing in the background. When he stroked the broadcloth, there was a faint purring

sound. When he fitted the coat to the customer's shoulders, the final pat was a caress.

Soon the customers were talking about that "new young man" at Glick's, and many insisted he wait on them. The proprietor was delighted. He rewarded Dad typically—for many years he underpaid him. Then, shrewdly sensing that the emergence of the automobile would carry his customers to brighter lights in larger cities, he sold Dad his store.

That's a bit unfair, since all the years of Dad's ownership were not that bad. There were those Saturday nights right after World War I when returning veterans, pockets stuffed with cash earned in the mud and blood of Chateau Thierry, eagerly bought the $10 pink silk shirts reposing in the showcase. The store was profitable; the Farmers Deposit Bank was getting its mortgage money; our family was well-fed and clothed and enjoying such luxuries as a quart of Chiesa's ice cream on Sunday night.

Dad never put back enough to buy the store himself, but picked up a partner, a moneyed dentist who, working in pre-Novocain days, found the business of extracting molars from screaming children too much for his nerves. As a clothing salesman, Dr. Mather was a good dentist, but he knew a supersalesman when he saw one, and was content to specialize in the haberdashery and let Dad handle the big-ticket items.

If some of us swallow hard at the suggestion of a four-day week, it's because we recall farmers working from dawn to late summer dusk, and Dad doing a 7-to-9 shift daily, extending to midnight on Saturdays. Then, there were so many "extras."

I remember the phone jangling after midnight and Dad rushing to answer. Our night watchman, Slick Shoup, picked up a monthly gratuity from local merchants for trying door handles to see if all was secured. This night there was a light on in the store basement. We could have guessed the light was left on by a careless clerk, but the store was his end and all, and Dad sleepily trudged uptown to confirm it. Mother resented these intrusions. I can hear her yet: "Humph, Slick has a passkey. He could have taken care of it and let you sleep. Probably afraid to go down there by himself."

If Dad loved merchandise, he loved people more, and that holds more secrets of salesmanship than the best tome Dale Carnegie ever turned out. His mission in life was to make his customers look their best. They sensed this, and not a few were more concerned about what *he* thought about that snazzy double-breasted than how it looked to them in the mirror.

If Dad loved merchandise, he loved people more; his mission in life was to make his customers look their best.

The store pulled customers from the farms and smaller farm communities. One small town nearby brought customers that provided special excitement. The town was Magnetic Springs, a spa of sorts that acquired a reputation for magnetic waters. To a healthy boy, this meant descending the stone steps to a cool cavern below and dipping your knife blade into the ever-bubbling waters. The blade was forever magnetized, and what fun to see pips stick to the knife blade or otherwise show off in ways that delight little boys.

However, to adults crippled by arthritis (we called it "rheumatism" those days), Magnetic Springs offered hope for the afflicted. At one time the tiny hamlet boasted three combination hotels and hospitals that in summer months were packed with pain-ridden people hoping to find relief by drinking the water and using the baths the hospitals provided.

If Dad did not recognize a customer, his conversational opening was, "Are you visiting the Springs?" Usually the stranger was. Dad knew they loved to talk about their symptoms. Captivated by his infinite capacity to listen and his unhurried approach to the sale, even on a busy Saturday night, they usually walked away from him, arms loaded with merchandise, and feeling better mentally if not physically. If the magnetic waters had not helped, their few minutes with a sympathetic listener did.

Most customers said the magnetic waters helped, but there were dissidents. The most notable was the customer who came hobbling into the store one night on crutches. He was obviously an unhappy man, so Dad, besides introducing himself and extending the usual pleasantries, pulled out all stops to create a relaxed atmosphere. When the tension persisted, Dad tried the usual punch line: "Are you feeling better by bathing at the Springs?"

The customer's scowl deepened. "Lord, no," he said. "You see these crutches? When I arrived there, I could walk."

As noted earlier, A.I. Glick saw the handwriting. Came the motorcar, the depressed '20s, and to many small-town merchants like Dad, it was the end of the line. My recurring nightmare is seeing the professionals from Dayton coming into town to clean out the store, much of the merchandise musty and out-of-style, at 20 cents on the dollar.

But the story has a relatively happy ending. Other than nagging arthritis, Dad enjoyed good health until his passing. Not many men were fishing on Lake Erie one week before they slept away at 85.

Some weeks after the store closed forever, Dad joined the jobless seeking work as extras during the Christmas season at a Columbus department store. They took Dad on as temporary help, but the old pro knew better. The magic still worked. His liking for people and instinct to please them licked the age barrier. His last position, and one of his happiest, was in a department store in a smaller community nearby where he finally took "early retirement" at age 83.

Our pastors tell us that, at the Golden Gate, it's what's in our hearts, not what's on our backs, that counts, but if there's a place for clothing stores, there's a place for this salesman. Customers who saw his smile and sampled his service seldom said "No." ❖

Officer Delahanty, Neighborhood Cop

By William Murphy

That was his name and he was assigned to the local station house in the neighborhood where I lived—"Southie," that section of Boston rightfully termed South Boston.

Perhaps Officer Delahanty was not unique back in the early '20s, but in today's world he certainly would stand out.

Physically, he was totally unlike the young men we see in police uniforms today who are lithe and strong, and drive cruise cars armed with two-way radios and all. No, Officer Delahanty was, in fact, a bit overweight and close to 60 years old. His upper lip was fringed with a graying mustache heavily tinged with the yellow stains of chewing tobacco.

He walked a beat, as did all officers, and checked in with the station at regular intervals by means of blue-painted metal boxes mounted on telephone poles that contained a telephone connected to the station house. He did not carry a pistol. He had a whistle, a set of handcuffs and a wooden "billy," which was later called a nightstick.

He walked his daily beat slowly, observing even the most minute of happenings around him. It was his manner, his approach to his job that earned him respect—and sometimes fear—from kids and the occasional adult.

Officer Delahanty made it his business to know every family on his beat. He could tell you who was gravely ill, which women were pregnant, who were and weren't churchgoers. He knew which men he could expect to arrest for drunkenness, and which ladies were wont to "rush the growler" (an Irish expression for the ladies who got a pail of beer from the ladies' window at the local tavern and carried it home under their capes). He could advise as to who was the most lenient confessor at the Gate of Heaven Catholic Church, as well as which nun was the toughest teacher.

Perhaps best of all was that he knew every kid on his beat. He knew which were troublemakers and which didn't need a close eye turned their way. And he had his own way of dealing with the former.

When a kid pulled a prank within his view, Office Delahanty knew he was physically unable to chase and catch the culprit, so he called out, "Maybe I can't run, but I can schnake (sic)!" And that he did. When the offender got home, he invariably found out that Officer Delahanty had been there before him and informed the parents of the misdeed; and of course, punishment followed.

My own brother, Joe, and his buddy, Ed, were often the target of Officer Delahanty's attention. Both boys seemed to get a kick out of throwing rocks through the neighborhood houses' windows. Of course, Delahanty got the news to their parents right away, with the usual results. (Oddly enough, Joe grew up and, in time, joined the Boston police force, where he served in perhaps the highest crime district for almost 25 years.)

Kids and adults have different views of right and wrong today, and, of course, policemen and crime control methods have had to change in order to cope with the world we live in. They say we shouldn't look back, but in many ways, the Delahanty days were special. ❖

possessed radios for news bulletins. What I did with my hot-off-the-press papers was keep those transient folks in touch with the world for mere pennies. The daily newspapers were 5 cents each and netted me 2 cents' profit. On the best days, I could sell maybe 33 papers for a grand profit of 66 cents. A 66-cent fortune on 66!

My carefully selected business spot was at a point where a stop sign brought Route 66 traffic to a temporary halt. "Paper, Mister?" or "Paper, Ma'am?" I asked thousands of drivers, and quite a few replied, "Sure," and tendered the nickel.

Also nearby was a popular and much-advertised restaurant. Highway billboards were amiable advertising companions beside major roads in those days, and many billboards strongly advertised visiting Clinton for home cooking at the finest restaurant between Lake Michigan and Santa Monica. The restaurant paid for the billboards, but by rights they could have asked me to help because the restaurant's business was my business, too. Every traveler who stopped for food was politely invited to invest 5 cents in the world's supreme bargain—that day's news. I had a lot more time for salesmanship with the travelers entering the restaurant, and they bought a lot more papers than those at stop signs.

A special gimmick I employed to intrigue tourists and get their attention was to tell them I collected matchbook covers and to ask if they had any they could

As a 66 entrepreneur at the age of 10, I loved the highway and viewed with awe and admiration the drivers and their cars rushing down it daily in both directions.

spare from interesting places. Many generously emptied their pockets and glove compartments. Some even took my name and address and sent me matchbook covers they methodically acquired during the rest of their journeys. That matchbook collection earned me a vast amount of exciting mail from all over the United States and allowed me to travel widely right there at one point on Route 66.

As a 66 entrepreneur at the age of 10, I loved the highway and viewed with awe and admiration the drivers and their cars rushing down it daily in both directions. I wanted wheels of my own and a chance to become one with 66 and boldly explore whatever lay down that mysterious, inviting ribbon of road.

Eventually I did journey on Highway 66 from one end to the other. That was a rewarding experience, yet somehow it lacked the speculative magic of that boyhood time in the 1930s when I peddled daily papers to tourists and did all of my traveling via the endless and pothole-free highway of the imagination.

There on Route 66, meeting the motoring pilgrims and supplying their papers, I learned firsthand that eager imagination always has no-cost tickets available anywhere in America or the world, and that reservations, passports, credit cards and cash are never needed.

Old Route 66 is gone now, except in Steinbeck, television reruns and American history. It was replaced by the wide, fast, impersonal interstates that purposely avoid small towns.

Gone, too, is that boyhood newsstand at a strategic pausing point beside the great east-and-west boulevard of Middle and Western America. Nobody, I'm sorry to say, gets kicks today—or buys nickel papers from an ambitious newsboy—on Route 66, other than in a vivid imagination.

Yet memories are strong and keep those good times and places richly and

robustly alive. Thus, Route 66 survives, travelers endlessly continue their journeys, and the newsboy still offers the headlines.

"Paper, Mister? Paper, Ma'am? Better learn what's happening in your world."

Sometimes it's fun to remember past happenings and to recapture other days. That's how it is for me, many jobs and years later, revisiting that jolliest of jobs—and getting my kicks on Route 66. ❖

That Old-Time Newsroom Frenzy

By Helen K. Cook

"Get a horse!" comedian Ed Wynn used to exhort listeners every Sunday night on the popular Texaco radio show.

He couldn't adjust to the automobile age and was hanging on to his buggy whip stock.

I, too, have this get-a-horse obsession when it comes to microchips and word processors. I used to lust after Jessica Fletcher's clackety typewriter on which she batted out the last chapter of *Murder, She Wrote*.

Hers is that old-fashioned kind of upright that makes hypnotic noises and spurs creativity like nothing else can. It's much like the one I used on my first job as a reporter for *The Maryville* (Missouri) *Daily Forum* in the late '30s.

The tapping of typewriters was but one contrapuntal mix of sounds that assaulted our ears all day.

Invariably, the rheumatic old Underwood stiffened up overnight. Every morning I had to type "The quick brown fox jumped nimbly over the lazy dog's back" several times before it would work.

During this warm-up period, I was inspired by the editor's energy and bounce. Chet wore his green eyeshade at a rakish angle and smoked cigars. His desk was William Randolph Hearstian in size, if not swank, and its surface was a jungle of paperwork.

Not so inspirational were the dilapidated office furnishings. Cobwebbed shelves held bound copies of *The Forum* from years back. A rickety bookcase sagged under the weight of beat-up encyclopedias, outdated world almanacs, newspapers from other towns and assorted cuts and photographs.

The tapping of typewriters was but one contrapuntal mix of sounds that assaulted our ears all day. We fleshed out our stories to the accompaniment of composing room uproar and the steady cacophony of Linotypes.

Charlie and Bonnie, operators of these formidable machines, commanded awe and respect. The tall, top-heavy behemoths had about 5,000 moving parts—all sorts of cams, rods, pulleys, levers and gears. The operators punched a keyboard that transformed a built-in pot of molten lead into solid lines of type. Now and then a sharp cry of pain rose above the din, meaning Charlie or Bonnie had been spattered with hot lead belched from the innards of the monster.

The Linotypes' racket was mild, though, compared with the back-room bedlam. Today's guardian EPA probably would have moved in and closed down what sounded like a combined foundry, blacksmith shop and wrecking ball.

Harlan, who was in charge of this tumult, sweated profusely as he tended fire under the cast-iron tub of the same pewtery muck that circulated through the Linotypes. This laborious process produced the cuts, or pictures, the advertising manager needed that day. Syndicated matter such as cartoons also had to be transformed into cuts.

Two heavy iron plates held the mats in place while the white-hot liquid was poured in. The metal hardened minutes later, the clamps were released and the sizzling bars yanked out. They hit the floor with percussive booms.

Then followed the shriek of rotating saws on metal to separate cuts, trim off excess and square up corners. After the press run, the casting metal was dumped into the tub and melted down again the next day.

Welcome respite from the noise came when I set out in the company car. My run included the college, churches, schools, the hospital and whatever I could pick up on the street.

Subscribers loved personals such as "Bill and Hank Slocum of Guilford transacted business in Maryville today." Visitors from nearby towns who loafed on benches in the courthouse square were always "transacting business" in the columns of *The Forum*.

Because of the vast territory I covered, anyone else who needed the car had to check with me. This might have gone to my head, but the austere paycheck—$12.50 a week— kept me humble.

Each morning, as the old Dodge lurched into high gear, everyone along Main Street knew I was off to get the news. Typical events that summer included the Skidmore punkin show, the rural letter carriers convention, a tornado that tore up the east end of town, a little girl who swallowed an open safety pin, and the crash-landing of a boy's homemade glider. Both the boy and the girl survived.

Jim Dorsey sent a ripple of show-biz excitement through town when he visited a local tycoon. He was my first celebrity. Dizzy with excitement, I skipped lunch and used the time to think of provocative questions. For one, I came up with, "Should jitterbugging be exterminated?"

His cornflower-blue eyes twinkled. "I wouldn't want to hurt any feelings," he said, "but it does seem that jitterbugs are necessary to the modern dance."

The interview had been delayed until the famed orchestra leader finished a golf game. It was late when I returned to the office flaunting an autographed photo. I managed to whip up this scoop before the deadline, but just barely.

I could always shut my mind to the shoproom noises, but the telephones couldn't be ignored.

Phones rang constantly. The town had two ex-changes—the Farmers and the Hanamo. Users on the Farmers line were mostly—well, farmers. Listings in the Hanamo book were city folks. Few people could afford the luxury of two exchanges. But *The Forum* couldn't operate without both.

A free farm-to-market message center evolved as a sideline. Over the static-filled country network, requests of this sort crackled in our ears:

"Would you call Mrs. Miller that I've got her dressed chickens ready?"

"Get Wadley on the phone and tell him I gotta have that harness fixed by tomorrow."

"Call Dr. Braniger 'cause I can't make it in today." (He was a dentist.)

Sometimes a call was for information. "Is it safe to hang out my wash?"

In those Depression days, *The Forum* didn't splurge on leased wire service, but the society editor was a whiz at shorthand. Daily, at 1 p.m., Doris sharpened her pencil and put on head-phones to await the crucial call from the United Press. Doris was unflappable, no matter how dire the news from afar. Quickly she transcribed her notes while the Linotypes stood by at a full rolling boil. Chet raced with the headline count.

By midafternoon, the back-room noises abated, replaced by peaceful low rumbles of the flatbed press. About 4 o'clock copies were passed around, still warm with the addictive aroma of printer's ink. Over coffee at the café next door, I basked in the thrill of reading words I had written, marveled at the daily miracle of bringing order out of chaos. Behind the chronicles of triumph and tragedy, in neat columns of print, lay piles of ink-smeared proof strips and scatterings of staff copy assailed by Chet's ferocious black pencil.

I looked forward to the renewed flurry of activity the next day, and the noise.

Now that old-time newsroom frenzy is only a memory. No more big bang casting of cuts. High-tech phototypesetting is quiet and efficient.

Typewriters have been replaced by video display terminals. How can stories leap to life from the passive circuitry of these deadpan contraptions that have no pulse?

There's something about the clatter of type-writer keys and the physical act of making it happen that anoints the mental process, builds confidence and causes thoughts to tap out in orderly progression.

Nevertheless, the battle of the old upright is clearly lost. Just as Ed Wynn's horse-and-buggy bias did nothing to rein in the automobile age, my stubborn attachment to an obsolete piece of equipment is equally futile.

Relentlessly the news will churn out. Good writing will emerge. But sadly missing in the electronic drone of today's workplace is the exhilarating sound and fury of batting out copy on a rheumatic old Underwood. ❖

A Matter of Trust

By Harry L. Armstrong

Hey, kid! Want to earn a dime?" Such was my introduction to Fred Snow, proprietor of Snow's Clothing Store. The year was 1927 and it was my first year at the high school in Bridgewater, Mass. I had been there only a few days, and was walking down the street on my lunch break. I hardly knew my way around the schoolhouse and knew less of the town.

It was a surprise to be approached in this manner, but I was interested. Times were good in 1927, but so were dimes. Having a country boy's innate distrust of city slickers—the population of Bridgewater was nearing 3,000, while my hometown of Halifax boasted fewer than 500 citizens—I approached warily.

"What's the catch?" I wanted to know.

"No catch," replied Mr. Snow, "I just want someone to take this envelope to the bank for me." As I hesitated, he held out the envelope and a dime at the same time. "There is $150 here, and after you deposit it, will you please bring back the receipt?"

If Mr. Snow were still doing business at the same place, I doubt that he would hand his bank deposit to a stranger. At the time, however, it was not unusual. Over the years I have met some people who were suspicious and distrustful, but my happier memories are of the people who looked me in the eye and said, "OK."

"Just pay what you can, when you can." With those few words, Art Shaw and I completed the first of many agreements that were to follow over the next several years. My wife and I had gone into his store for the first time that evening and had selected a refrigerator we wanted, but could not afford if he expected cash. Later we would buy other things, including radios and our very first television set. I had agreed to his conditions at our first meeting, and Mr. Shaw, believing me, saw no need for contracts and signatures.

If you think that gasoline was hard to come by during the "fuel shortage" of the '70s, you should have run out of gas in a strange city in 1944. That was the situation one day when my pickup gasped and died as I was proceeding through the outskirts of Boston. I was carrying neither ration coupons nor money. I suppose that I could have found some way to place a collect call to my employers who then could have sent someone 40-odd miles to rescue me, but as master mechanic for Thomas Brothers, I was supposed to be a problem solver, not a problem causer.

Remembering that I had passed a gas station no more than a quarter-mile back, I set out on foot. Entering the station, two things caught my attention: a rather stern-looking individual sitting at a desk, and a crudely lettered sign on the wall behind him that stated bluntly, "$5 DEPOSIT ON GAS CANS."

Stifling my impulse to ask directions to the rest room, from whence I could sneak away quietly, I came right to the point. "I need at least 5 gallons of gas, and I have neither coupons nor money. Also, I need a can to carry the gas to my pickup, which is parked up the street out of gas." At this point I debated as to whether or not I should mention my employers; contractors, as a group, were not generally regarded as blue-chip credit risks. I decided to continue, "As road-building contractors, we have plenty of coupons, and I will have the office mail you the coupons and a check in the morning."

For about a minute I stood there, slightly uncomfortable, while the station manager looked me up and down. The stern look dissolved into sort of a smile as he said, "I guess that will be OK, but you bring that can back right away, you hear?"

I went through the '20s, '30s and '40s trusting and being trusted. ❖

My Museum of Restaurant Slanguage

By Francis L. Fugate

I never see a waitress, pencil poised over her pad, that I don't shed a tear for the passing of restaurant slang, one of America's most colorful institutions. We need a living museum in which the vernacular of the past can be preserved for the enjoyment and enlightenment of present and future generations. Historical dictionaries just don't communicate the flavor of speech.

I long once more to have a waitress approach, armed with nothing than a cheery "What'll it be?" and her memory. When I order wieners and sauerkraut, a baked potato, and the lettuce-and-tomato salad without dressing, it would do my heart good to hear her raise a stentorian voice toward the kitchen: *"Dogs in the hay, Mrs. Murphy in a sealskin coat, bunny grub and love apples—hold the soppin's!"* The cook would echo the call.

> *At the conclusion of the main dish I would order Jell-O just to see if she called it "nervous pudding," "shimmy" or "shivering Liz."*

At the conclusion of the main dish I would order Jell-O just to see if she called it "nervous pudding," "shimmy" or "shivering Liz."

I was awed by her memory, which enabled an experienced waitress to call out a dozen orders from random positions along a counter, all the while bantering with her customers, and infallibly bring each to the correct person. When the diner finished eating, she would scribble the amount of the check on a chit without having to chew her pencil and squint at the menu. But those days have been replaced by steamy, plastic-shrouded cafeteria tables, printed order forms with squares to check ("no substitutions"), and computerized cash registers that beep and grind to inform the cashier in lighted numerals how much change she should give you.

The origin of restaurant slang, or "riddle language," as etymologists call it, is obscured in a misty past. Some say that cooks refused to understand waitresses who did not pay them to learn the jargon. Undoubtedly, some waitresses paid their dues to join the quick-lunch fraternity, but the verbiage pre-dated the '20s and '30s, when it was most prevalent in the United States. Many of the terms had their roots far back in Great Britain. For example, "Murphy"—for potato— dates to the mid-18th century; "love apple" came from the 16th century, based on the supposed aphrodisiac qualities of tomatoes, and "bunny grub" for lettuce or green vegetables started as schoolboy slang at Cheltenham College during the mid-19th century.

The practice probably originated with costermongers who sold foodstuffs on the streets and in stalls, particularly at fairs. They depended upon the cleverness of their patter to attract business. Certainly the old-time circus hawker who chanted, *"Peacorn, popnuts, sodagum and chewing-water—buy 'em in a bottle, in a bag, in a box!"* garnered more dimes than his inexperienced competitor who merely enumerated his wares.

My first experience with restaurant slang came one morning when my father took me to breakfast at his favorite diner. The waitress smiled at Dad. "The usual?" she asked. He nodded.

"Graveyard stew for the molly-coddle and a mug of murk—no cow!" she roared toward the kitchen.

My father was particular about his milk toast. He wanted the toast done to a golden brown, buttered, then sprinkled with cinnamon before hot milk was poured over it. Of course, he never contaminated coffee with cream.

I wanted pancakes and a glass of milk. Dad cautioned the waitress that I would eat only two pancakes but use a lot of syrup.

"A short stack, heavy on the Vermont. Draw one moo juice!"

The slang varied from one part of the country to another, but drummers quickly spread the vernacular as they traveled from territory to territory and swapped experiences

with other salesmen. The West was most distinctive. There, waitresses inevitably known as "biscuit shooters" or "cookie pushers" had to translate the vernacular which cowboys brought from the range. When in town, cowhands headed for the "beanery," "feed-bag" "grub house," or "swallow-and-get-out trough" for "fluff duffs" or "soft grub," as they called hotel or fancy food.

Pancakes were "hen-fruit stir" or "splatter dabs," drowned in molasses known as "blackstrap," "larrup," "lick" or "long sweetenin'." Molasses was the universal sweetener of the range. Sugar was so rare that one cowboy, on being offered sugar, said, "No, thanks; I never use salt in my coffee." Doughnuts, also a rarity on the range, were called "bear-sign." Coffee was "Arbuckles" (after the favorite brand of the West), "brown gargle," "jamoka" or "belly-wash" if it was weak.

In the early days, when the West was made up of territories, homesteaders were few and far between. The few chickens they raised produced only enough eggs for their own tables. Eggs were dubbed "state's eggs" because they had to be shipped out from the states. Some turned out to be "souvenirs"—too old to be eaten.

Biscuits were "hot rocks," "sinkers" or "sourdough bullets." Butter to go on the biscuits was "axle grease," "cow grease" or "skid grease." A butter substitute made of syrup or sorghum mixed with bacon grease was called "Charlie Taylor," and not as a compliment to Charlie Taylor, whoever he may have been.

Beef steak, if tough, as was usually the case, was "machinery belting," and the gravy that disguised its stringy texture was "immigrant butter," "sop" or "Texas butter."

The only pork available was salt pork or sowbelly: "pig's vest with buttons," "sow bosom," or "Kansas City fish," if it was fried.

Side dishes inevitably included rice, "John Chinaman" or "swamp seed"; tomatoes stewed with bread and sugar, "pooch"; beans, "prairie strawberries" or "whistleberries"; and sweet potatoes, "music roots."

The blue-plate special was usually topped off with a dish of boiled rice and raisins: rice pudding on the menu but "horse-thief's special" or "spotted pup" to the cowboy. If he wanted it covered with a viscous sauce made of sugar, flour and water, he asked for "dip," the same name he applied to the powerful antiseptic used to kill lice and ticks on cattle. However, when he got to town, the cowboy preferred pie for dessert, "boggy-top" if it was open-faced. If lemon meringue was available, he would usually order "a slab of that one with the calf slobbers on top."

If I ever get my Living Museum of Restaurant Slanguage, it will portray an open-all-night quick-lunch counter, vintage 1935. The time will be 7 in the morning, when the graveyard shift is getting off and ordering "supper" and those going to work are eating breakfast.

There will be the inevitable signs on the wall: "In God We Trust, All Others, CASH," and "Don't kick at our coffee. You may be old and weak, too, someday." The menu will be chalked on a large slate. When the tableau comes to life, the waitress will alternate between taking orders and delivering them. A gum-chewing cashier will leave the cash register long enough to serve drinks.

The dialogue will go like this:

"Hi ya, big boy! What'll it be?"

"Give me a couple of crullers and a cup of black coffee."

"Trot out a team of grays! Draw one in the dark! What's yours, sport?"

"Poached eggs on toast, sweetheart, and coffee."

"Adam and Eve on a raft and cup o' mud! How about you? Did you work up an appetite last night?"

"Did I! I'll have the ham, potatoes and cabbage."

"Noah's boy with Murphy carrying a wreath! Anything to drink?"

"Just water. I've been drinking coffee all night."

"One on the city! And how about you, Harry?"

"Maude, I'll take the hash with baked beans."

"Yesterday, today and forever, with a million on a platter! Say, haven't seen you for an age. Did the railroad send you to China?"

"No, I've been in bed with the grippe."

"Jeez, too bad. What'll you have?"

"Bacon and eggs."

"Pair o' headlights and a string o' flats for the engineer! How about—"

"Hey, sweetheart, where's my poached eggs?"

"Rush the biddies on a raft! How about you, fellow?"

"Beef stew and a cup of tea, I think."

"Bossy in a bowl—boiled leaves on the side! Al, you look like you have been dragged through a knothole."

"Heck of a night, Maude. I'm pooped. Got any oysters?"

"Fresh in last night."

"Give me a dozen raw and a glass of buttermilk."

"Twelve alive in the shell and a billiard!"

"How's the corned beef and cabbage, Honey?"

"The cook personally stole the recipe from Mr. Waldorf and Mr. Astor."

"Guess I'll chance it."

"La Bullie Hibernain! And I missed you, didn't I?"

"The steak for me—rare."

"Slab of moo—let him chew! What can I get for the best taxi pusher in town?"

"Couple of sinkers and a cup of coffee with just a little cream."

"Two submarines and a scuttle of java with a streak of bovine extract! How are you this morning, Winston?"

"Too tired to work, but I'm on my way to the salt mine. Gimme ham an' eggs."

"Roast two on a slice of squeal. And yours?"

"I'll take two pork chops on the special."

"Lay a couple of Hebrew enemies on a blue plate! Which dessert do you want?"

"The ice cream on rice pudding."

"Ice the rice! You're next, Pops."

"Two eggs, and I want them turned over."

"Fry two and flop 'em!"

"And could I get a cup of hot chocolate?"

"Man wants a black cow! Mister, you've been sitting here looking hungry too long. What'll you have?"

"A bowl of tomato soup, a plate of beans, bread and butter, a piece of apple pie, and a glass of water."

"One splash of red noise, platter of Saturday nights, dough well done with cow to cover, Eve with the lid on, and a chaser of Adam's ale!" ❖

Additional Terms From the Quick-Lunch Era

Beans—ammunition, coal miner's strawberries, forty-fives, free-holies

Butter—lubricant, mortar, plaster, putty, salve, smear, spread, stucco, Vaseline.

Catsup—blood, cat-soup, communist, red lead.

Corned beef and cabbage—crippled beef on a load of hay, Dinty Moore, Jiggs and Fried

Eggs—bride and groom, two looking at you, two with their eyes open.

Grapefruit—eyeful.

Ham or bacon and eggs—cackle berries and grunt.

Hash—the great unknown, kitchen mystery, plate of mystery.

Jelly—fly-catcher.

Pepper—fly specks, high-stepper, pep, snee-zoning.

Salt—Lot's wife, sand, sea dust.

Stew—Black Mike, bum's special, kitchen mystery, mulligan.

Tea—scandal broth (British import).

I Was a "Slave" in the Dime Store

By Irene Steigerwald

It was at the end of the much-touted "Roaring '20s" that we also started a "roaring" Depression. Work was scarce. By dint of much finagling, a relative who had connections managed to wrangle me a job in the dime store. This magnificent employment paid 30 cents an hour, but I was deliriously happy to get it.

At that time, the five-and-ten was really a five-and-ten. There were no television sets, lawn mowers or expensive articles of clothing for sale. You might find something priced at 98 cents, but that was about the limit.

On the first day I reported for duty, I found that I was expected to leave my purse in the office. Presumably this was so that we would not walk away with any valuables. (*In the dime store?* I thought.)

I felt very rebellious about this because I felt if I needed my hankie or comb, I should be able to get it. Being a city child, something else occurred to me: How did I know *they* wouldn't take something from *me*? After all, there was a Depression going. However, I reluctantly handed the purse over into their safekeeping and said nothing.

I was given the usual application form, and when I got down to question No. 4, I read, "What would you like to do as your life work?" Foolishly, I told the truth. "I would like to write stories."

Later on, I was assigned to the cosmetics counter to sell soap. The callow young floorwalker wasted no time in giving me the business.

"Selling soap is a lot different from writing stories, isn't it?" he would simper whenever he passed my counter.

Besides the many young females who came to purchase cosmetics, I had a steady customer who puzzled me. This was a dirty old fellow who could be described in only one way: He was a bum. I couldn't understand why he kept purchasing Bay Rum Hair Tonic, since it was obvious that nothing—but nothing—ever went on his hair.

Day after day, he would sidle furtively up to my counter, push a dime across the glass, snatch up a bottle of hair tonic and dart out the door. This item became my best seller—in fact, I was constantly sold

> *At that time, the five-and-ten was really a five-and-ten. You might find something priced at 98 cents, but that was about the limit.*

out. The same snide young floorwalker explained it to me. "He drinks it!" he said, and forbade me to sell the old fellow any more.

Our counters were very narrow and the space where we stood was only a couple of feet wide. This could be disastrous if you happened to draw a working partner who was broad in the beam. It entailed much grunting and pushing to get past each other, and if the cash register drawer was open, you had a major crisis. At 98 pounds, I used to pray that they wouldn't hire any fat workers.

Since I had been hired as a "floater," I worked everywhere in the store, but I hated working at the oilcloth counter. This department was managed by a tall, somber girl who was as oily as her cloth.

To make matters worse, the flies *loved* this counter. During July and August they swarmed in and clung to the rolls of oilcloth with sticky

delight. This was long before air conditioning, of course.

The genius who discovered the hanger-type arrangement for measuring oilcloth had not yet been born; we used a yardstick and a pair of scissors. This yardstick proved to be a weapon in my energetic little hands. I was constantly apologizing for poking passing customers in the eye, or swiping them across the back as I busily went about my measuring and cutting.

In due course, I graduated from oilcloth and was promoted to making, or rather filling, cream puffs in the store window. This was supposed to be good advertising. I was provided with a table, about 600 empty cream-puff shells, and a mountainous tub of whipped cream. The idea was to fill a huge, udder-type bag with whipped cream; then, pointing it at a defenseless cream puff, I squeezed and hoped for the best.

I suffered an agony of embarrassment because I had a constant audience of college boys in front of the window, and they delighted in taunting me. They would give me advice regarding my work and technique as they surveyed me through the glass, and would "moo" encouragingly if I managed to hit the cream-puff hole.

At noon we spent our time in what was laughingly known as the ladies' "lounge." This was a small, drab room, sparsely furnished with old, prickly wicker furniture, upon which I would defy anyone to actually lounge. However, we did manage to put our feet up. A picture of our benefactor hung on the wall in a highly ornate gilt frame. This frame was plastered with solid blobs of used chewing gum, which the wage slaves had placed there in gratitude for his munificence.

After lunch, I usually worked at the candy counter. Here we lifted and unloaded carton after carton of candy, gum and all kinds of sweets.

One day I was chopping a huge slab of milk chocolate to be weighed and bagged. We did the chopping with an ice pick. I made a vicious lunge at the candy and it slid from the counter and fell on my foot—all 25 pounds of it. As I bent over, mute with pain, the manager appeared on the scene and inquired acidly what I thought I was doing. He picked up the slab of chocolate, reprimanded me for getting it dirty and brushed it off, placing it back on the counter for sale.

Nothing was said about my foot, which had assumed the proportions of a balloon.

This store also had a sheet-music department. It was customary for a pianist to play the selections which the customer wished to hear before purchasing. On the days when the regular pianist was absent, it fell to me to play these little numbers.

Yes, Sir, That's My Baby proved not too difficult. I also got through *Ain't She Sweet?* and a few other saccharine ditties. My downfall came about when a group of my chums showed up and requested *Hungarian Rhapsody*. I launched into it with enthusiasm that shook the china off nearby shelves and brought my nemesis, the floorwalker, who wanted to know if I thought I was in Carnegie Hall. This ended my career as a performing artist for a while.

The manager had a queer penchant for changing the displays from one end of the counter to the other at the drop of a hat. I would no sooner erect a huge pyramid of cans, bottles and tubes than he would appear from his lair at the rear of the store and demand that they be shifted to the opposite corner of the counter.

The manager had a queer penchant for changing the displays from one end of the counter to the other at the drop of a hat.

It was not unusual for the display to travel to all four corners of the counter in the course of one work day. I believe this came under the heading of keeping our morale up, or the assumption that we must "look busy."

Things are very different now, I know. The counters and aisles are generally wide and roomy. No manager in his right mind would dare to ask a worker to change a display five seconds after the closing bell. Workers have "rights" and unions to preserve them, and I suppose that is all to the good.

Nevertheless, something is missing. Dime stores are busy places, but the spirit of gaiety is gone, and so is the *esprit de corps* that aligned "us," the workers, against "him," the boss, in a harmless game of matching wits.

The other day I went into the five-and-ten to buy some glassware. The queenly creature who deigned to wait on me couldn't have cared less. As I watched her thumping and wrapping with complete disregard for the glass, I thought of myself as I had been—the eagerest of beavers as I braced my then-scrawny shoulder against the wheel of industry.

There's no doubt about it. Workers never had it so good, and they have it more convenient in a hundred ways.

But we had more fun! ❖

The Cobbler's Shop

By Mrs. William A. Prescott

All winter we wore black leather high-laced shoes. I took new ones to bed with me; I loved their smell. We laced these up and wound the laces around the top and tied the ends in a bow in front. Mine met in the middle about four holes up, and then a gap began to spread and got wider and wider. It narrowed down again, but pull as hard as I could, they never met in the middle.

I broke all my shoestrings pulling, and then I knotted the ends together and tried to conceal the knots. When there were three or more knots, I had difficulty getting the shoes on and off.

The soles were stitched on, but I soon wore the stitching thin so that the tip of the shoe was loose. It was fun to stick my pencil in these; I got the whole class laughing as I walked around in them. When they ripped further, the sole flapped at every step. That was the time to get the other sole flapping.

When the leather on the toes got scuffed, it could be peeled off liked burned skin. The boy beside me helped with this. He worked on one shoe while I worked on the other. Soon they were all gray and I covered them with black ink. We were sent to the hall many times for this. Here we squirted water from the water fountain at each other. They changed one of our seats regularly, but whoever sat near either of us got in trouble.

By this time, my flopping, knotted shoes were too much for Aunt Jen (I forgot to say my anklebones hit each other, too, so there was a hole on each side). She'd send me to the cobbler to have them repaired.

I'd leave them in Aunt Jen's name, V.B. Wilson. The cobbler misunderstood me and wrote Phoebe Wilson. I wore my Sunday shoes while the others were being repaired. When it was time to pick them up, Aunt Jen would say,

"You'd better get these good ones shined while you are there."

I am sure Aunt Jen never visited one of these shoe-shining places; had she known the position in which I sat to obtain the polish job, she would have been horrified.

But I loved it. I climbed up three big steps almost to the ceiling, and one on the other, he piled shoe boxes behind me so my legs would reach the foot things, which were a good 3 feet apart. This nearly split me in half, but with my short dress, I'm sure anyone could have had a view of my belly button. I grabbed the center front of my dress and hung on to the middle of the chair. This brought my head down to rest on my knees, giving me a good view of the cobbler as he worked.

He applied a gob of paste polish first, then worked it in with his bare hands. Wiping his hands on his already black apron, he then pushed two brushes back and forth with my foot between, and ended by rubbing them with a big cloth. They surely did shine.

The cobbler knew "Phoebe" now, and when I'd climbed off the high chair, he let me watch him mend shoes. He held small nails in his mouth and pulled them out as he needed them. A sanding machine smoothed the nails off. When I told him I had to file the nails on my shoes when they poked through, he said, "Now, Phoebe, don't you do that. When they need filing, come down and do it here."

I did, too. Nights when my friends had music lessons or dentist appointments and there was nowhere to go but home, I visited my friend the cobbler, sanded my nails down, and helped.

I couldn't make up my mind which I wanted to do when I grew up—be a clerk at the jewelry counter in the 5-and-10-cent store, or massage shoes with soft black paste and whiz those brushes back and forth. ❖

My Father, the Druggist

By Marjorie Fisher Stekl

Yesterday I walked into a drugstore in Baraboo, Wis., just around the corner from where my father, Herman Fisher, and his two brothers had operated a drugstore that bore the Fisher name from 1888 until the early 1980s when it became a variety store.

How the role of the druggist has changed! I watched the druggist count a certain number of capsules from a bottle, put them in a box, label it and give the box to me. I remembered going into my father's store as a child and seeing him standing, mortar and pestle in front of him, a scale at one side, a measuring spoon nearby and a prescription in front of him as he worked. I knew I must keep silent until he had finished, sometimes for an hour.

I also look back on the hot summer days when my brother and I put labels on Fisher drugs that my father brewed and compounded in a laboratory over the store. Every fall, Uncle Frank took these products throughout the county by horse and buggy. Remedies such as Fisher's Health Restorer, Fisher's Cough Syrup, Fisher's Electric Liniment, Fisher's Carbolic Salve and Fisher's Corn Cure were welcomed for winter use by area farmers.

One hot August day when my perspiring father came downstairs after a day's work with remedies, Charley Ringling (of the famous Ringling Brothers Circus, a longtime friend of the family) happened to be in the store. "Herman, instead of having Frank take your products around the county, why don't you let him come with the circus and sell them there?" he asked my father. "You would make a lot more money."

After thinking it over, my father told Charley that drugs sold at circuses were not up to the Fisher standard, so he refused the offer.

Young Dr. Farnsworth said he feared he would have to leave, perhaps try Sauk City, as he wasn't making enough to pay the rent; office calls were 25 cents and house calls were 50 cents!

Before my parents' marriage in 1894, my father lived and slept over the store because, of course, a druggist must be available day and night! He told us of several amusing incidents that occurred at that time. The one I remember best happened one cold January night when my father heard pounding on the front door. After dressing and opening the door, he saw one of the town drunks. My father let him in and asked what he wanted.

"A clay pipe—and charge it," the man said. After receiving the pipe, he walked out the door without so much as a thank-you.

Another incident concerned a veterinarian who came to the store several times a week from a nearby town. He always asked to use the toilet, which was in the basement where the wine and liquor were kept. Strangely, some of the wine and liquor disappeared after each visit. Finally, one day when my father saw the veterinarian come in, he hurried downstairs and painted the mouth of each bottle with nitrate of silver. When the vet came upstairs he had a black rim around his mouth. Everyone began to laugh. He looked in the mirror and made a quick exit!

Soon after my parents were married, they moved into a newly built, nine-room house. My brother was born there in 1896 and I followed in 1897. My husband and I have lived in this house for almost 60 years, and it was our two daughters' home until their marriages. Now the eight grandchildren love to "come home." I still wonder how my father ever cared for the house. He put up and removed storm windows and screens, mowed the lawn and took care of a vegetable garden. Still he left for the store at 5 a.m. six days a week, came home only for dinner, and then left again to work until 11 p.m. or later. He rode a bicycle whenever possible. Many winter nights he was called back to the store to fill prescriptions when epidemics such as diphtheria, scarlet fever and "the grippe" struck Baraboo.

One would think that a busy druggist like my father would have no time for a hobby, but my father loved flowers and planted a thick row of hollyhocks that bordered our lot. He loved sweet peas and each spring planted several rows. It was my pleasant duty to pick a large bunch every Saturday and place them on the soda fountain at the store. For this service, I received a 5-cent chocolate ice-cream soda! One day, as I came with my flowers, my father

John Slobodnik

looked at me and said, "How you have grown, Honey. I think you are big enough for a 10-cent soda!" How happy I was!

I remember another story that illustrates my father's character. A young Sauk County farm boy had just graduated from medical college and asked my father if he could rent the rooms above the store to open his practice. My father agreed, as Baraboo needed another doctor. However, after a few months, young Dr. Farnsworth said he feared he would have to leave, perhaps try Sauk City, as he wasn't making enough to pay the rent; office calls were 25 cents and house calls were 50 cents!

My father had grown fond of the young doctor and realized he knew his medicine. So he told him to stay, and forget the rent until he was able to pay. I do not know how long it was until he was able to pay, but I do know he was in this same office until his death in the '30s, and that no Fisher was ever allowed to pay him for his services. He was most grateful for the help given him.

I look back with a great deal of joy at the winter of 1911–1912 and the following summer. The Baraboo druggists had met and decided to close their stores at noon on Sundays. At last, my brother and I got to know our father. He built a skating pond for us in the back yard, but the big surprise and joy came when he announced that he felt he could afford to buy a car! The automobile dealer let him bring home pictures of the Maxwell my father wanted. We all sat around the dining-room table to discuss our purchase. All accessories were extra, of course. Did we need a windshield? "Yes," my father said; otherwise bugs might fly in his face. Did we need doors? Not in front; my brother might have to jump out quickly to help hold a frightened horse. Back doors? Yes, Mother wanted to keep us cleaner. Side curtains? Our car was to be a

The big surprise and joy came when he announced that he felt he could afford to buy a car! Did we need a windshield? "Yes," my father said; otherwise bugs might fly in his face.

touring car, so yes, because we might have to put the top up if it rained.

One spring day, the dealership called to say our car was there. At the garage, Father was shown how to crank the car, where the accelerator was, the foot brake and the hand brake. Then he got in and drove the car home.

How could we eat our dinner without first having a ride in *our* car? So we all got in and rode around the block.

From then on, our Sundays were filled with drives in the country. Our favorite was the drive to Parie du Sac. Mother would pack a picnic lunch. She and I would put on our dusters and tie on our hats and she would admonish my father, "Please, Herman, don't go over 15 miles per hour. I want to enjoy the scenery." Only once did my brother have to jump out of the car to help hold a frightened horse as we drove by.

Coming home, we would stop to have our supper and let the engine cool at Kinschi's Spring, halfway up the bluff. If it had started to get dark, my brother and I would spit into a tube leading to the acetylene tank on the running board so gas would form to light the headlights on our way home.

There was only one "hurt" involved in the ownership of our car. We had one customer who came in every morning, took two expensive cigars out of the case, paying for neither, then stayed to visit with friends. One day he came in and said he wanted to close out his account because anyone who could afford to buy a car didn't need his business!

Our happy summer ended in October when, upon the urging of a Chicago surgeon, my father entered a hospital for a simple hernia operation. Months of illness followed and he died of an embolism on Jan. 6, 1913. Part of his obituary from the *Baraboo Republic* read: "Herman Fisher was a true friend to many" I would add, "And a wonderful father." ❖

JAY KILLIAN

The Old Neighborhood

Chapter Five

Quite a few years back, after Janice and I had moved back to the farm, we made a weekly trek to town for groceries and other supplies. Our route took us through one old neighborhood and past the home of a friend I really never knew.

I feel in some ways I knew him quite well. Almost every sunny day as we drove our old Ford toward town the elderly gentleman was there. Our friendly waves were returned with interest—smiles and a tip of his old flop hat. It was as if he thought he had some sort of obligation to be more than a little neighborly, as if there was responsibility in living, as the poet said, in "the house by the side of the road." We saw him giving other cars the same; this was truly "a friend of man."

For a long time it was the man and his wife—just like it was Janice and me. I told myself that we would have to stop by and chat with the couple. I could easily see the four of us becoming fast friends. He and I would talk about fishing, the garden and the weather. She and Janice would talk about canning, children and grandchildren. But we were always headed on into town and … well, you know.

So we always waved and smiled at them as we passed by, our friendship confined to a quarter-mile strip of street. We saw them out hoeing in her flower beds. We saw them walking hand in hand to the mailbox. We saw them swinging together on the old porch swing.

Then one day he was alone.

From that time on there was a melancholy touch to the old man's wave. Glancing down from the porch, he would smile and touch the brim of the flop hat. Our eyes would meet in the briefest of communion. Then I would be on down the street. I redoubled my resolve to stop by and meet him. I just needed the right excuse—something other than, "We were just passing by, and—"

For a couple of years he continued his ambassador-of-the-road status. He was confined to the old porch swing, from which he waved feebly.

Then he, too, was gone.

One day a handwritten sign was on the cornerpost of the driveway. Pulling over, we read it. "Thanks," it said, "to all who waved and honked to Dad. It kept him going for a long time. Dad passed away last Thursday. God bless you all."

In tears Janice and I pulled our car away from the driveway that we could have driven up so many times for so many years. I had lost a dear friend I never knew. All of the fishing trips we could have taken, the checkers we could have played, the tall tales we could have spun—none ever happened.

Janice and I resolved that day to not get in such a hurry again. We have tried in the ensuing decades to become better neighbors. More than anything, I decided that the spirit of my friend should not die. Now when anyone passes through our neighborhood, I wave. Whether it be neighbor or stranger, I tip my hat and smile a greeting. I do it all in honor and memory of a friend I never knew—a good friend from that Old Neighborhood in the Good Old Days.

—Ken Tate

Clothesline Reading

By Barbara Bullman Young

Poor Mr. West! I wonder when his wife will be well enough to get around."

"Debbie's home from camp."

"I see that the young couple by the delicatessen is expecting!"

How did my mother know these things about the neighbors just from looking out our back window in Brooklyn so long ago? Her art of "clothesline reading" gave her instant information about the neighbors and their activities. I imagine that he phrase "Don't show your dirty linen in public" was meant for our block! She saw Mr. Murphy's pants hanging on the line after a long absence; the Sullivan line had brand-new diapers strung out proudly; Mr. West was still hanging out the wash himself. (Mrs. West never would have left those big spaces or hung those shirts that way! They don't even look clean!) A whole summer of Debbie's camp clothes are displayed— looks like her mother will be busy mending this week. Maternity tops are hanging by the delicatessen line.

Of course, we didn't know most of the people on our crowded city block, but Mother knew something about them by "reading" their clotheslines. The close quarters encouraged the kind of familiarity not often known elsewhere.

There was very little visiting back and forth in our homes—most visiting was done on the stoops, on the avenue, and out the windows! I believe that in the city, even without a phone, we did more talking (and even more walking) and especially more hollering out the windows. I remember my long conversations while hanging out the front windows that faced the stoops. We lived on the second floor, and even when the bell rang, we always went to the window for a thorough interrogation before we trekked downstairs to open the door—if at all! Mother, however, usually exchanged most of her neighborhood gossip while hanging out the clothes from the open back window, while cold drafts chilled the back rooms.

We didn't know most of the people on our crowded city block, but Mother knew something about them by "reading" their clotheslines.

I can see it as plainly as if I were still there—the backyard scene in Brooklyn. It is a rectangular block of two-story brick houses all connected and backing on the central enclosed back yards. Each house's precious few yards (literally) are separated from each other with various kinds and colors of fencing and endless two-layered, crisscrossed clotheslines, bare in rain, stiff and shiny, or white in winter, and a live, flapping, multicolored patchwork in the wind and sun. When I was sick, I got to lie in my parents' bed during the day so I could look out the back window; I used to stare for hours at the rows of wash. I watched how they swayed in unison to the wind's tunes. A lone weathervane rooster perched on a nearby roof seemed to direct the dancing clothes as the wind changed direction.

My Swedish great-grandmother used to take in washing to supplement a meager widow's earnings. She was always so proud of her clean wash and enjoyed admiring it,

hanging in the sun. It was a job to be proud of in those days. After boiling the water and scrubbing each piece by hand with coarse, homemade soap in the old washtub, it was indeed an accomplishment!

Those were the days when "wash day" meant all day. They started early to take full advantage of the sunshine, and had to be ready to rush to the window to pull the clothes in if it started to rain.

Those who are dependent upon the clothesline and the weather have developed an elaborate, unwritten list of rules and regulations regarding the hanging out of wash. Appearances are very important! If you hang them just right, you cut down on ironing. Colors should be matched; undershirts get pinned in size places; socks should be paired and hung by the toe, and so forth and so forth. To leave the clothes out overnight is the sign of a careless housekeeper indeed!

Although my mother is clothesline-conscious, I am strictly utilitarian about hanging out

wash and the rules just amuse me. Being used to the handy electric dryer, I don't care how they look as long as they get dry. My mother is embarrassed and my mother-in-law appalled by the way I hang out clothes the few times I have to. My wash has been rehung for me more than once because, "What would the neighbors say if they could see this?"

In my neighborhood, the neighbors aren't close enough to see my back yard or call to me from the window. We do cherish our privacy, our surrounding woods and gardens, especially when the seasons change. Here, nature is our neighbor; when the houses are farther apart, sometimes the people are, too, in many ways. The outside of a house doesn't reveal much anyway about the people inside, especially the identically bricked fronts of the city tenements.

But the back yards reveal what we don't see much anymore, something of the people themselves, something that proves the individuality of those inside the imposing fa-cades. Those clotheslines stretching end to end for sun and neighbors to see tell more about the family than the neat lawns and ranch houses that sit in suburbia.

I hear that Brooklyn is changing, but I still miss some special things: the sound of the foghorn in the bay, the sudden whiff of a salty ocean breeze, and the clean, flapping wash to be seen from that back-room window and to be heard whispering in the breeze. Those clotheslines seemed to tie the houses together, and reveal them to be homes with families as individual as ours, who shared with us the same sun and wind—and even the same brand of shorts! ❖

My Kind of Town

By Paul Schilling

The Los Angeles, Calif., of today has too many cars, too many apartments, too much smog, too many people and too many bumper-to-bumper freeways. But it wasn't always that way.

Let me tell you of the Los Angeles I once knew when the sky above was clear and blue. You could see the big Hollywood sign on the Sierra Madre mountains for a distance of 20 miles. From the Baldwin hills, one could view Santa Monica Harbor and the beach towns of Venice and Ocean Park.

When I was a boy, Los Angeles was an area of gentle rolling hills, creeks and streams running southward to the La Ballona channel, then on to the sea.

Huckleberry Finn had nothing on us; we had swimming and good fishing holes, too. Can you imagine catching catfish, bluegill and crawdads in Los Angeles? It is hard to believe, but true.

Can you picture Los Angeles with corn, lima bean, watermelon, lettuce and celery fields? Believe me, that's the way it was. Just a mile or so from our house were acres of lima beans. Many times we went to the fields after the threshing machines passed through. We combed the ground for the beans that were hidden in the dirt. Mom was always glad to receive them in those days of the Depression.

One day, my dad came home from work and glanced at the pot of lima beans on the stove. My father was not one to take the Lord's name in vain, but he put his lunch pail down heavily and said, "Hebrews 13:8." If you are not familiar with that passage, it reads, "Jesus Christ, the same yesterday and today and forever."

In the year 1933, thousands of people began migrating to California from the Midwest to escape the dust storms and drought. "Sunny California, the land of milk and honey," they cried.

Families drove west in their jalopies loaded down with all of their household belongings, seeking work in the citrus belt of Southern California and the farms and ranches of the San Joaquin Valley.

Unscrupulous ranchers and farmers took advantage of these beggarly people and housed them in tents and shacks on the farms. Their wages were so low that by the time they paid for rent and food, there was nothing left. They couldn't move on; before long they were in debt to their employers.

Al Jolson belted out his famous *California, Here I Come*, and thousands more headed west. Bing Crosby crooned *I'm Gonna Make the San Fernando Valley My Home*, and several more thousand hit the road. Hundreds of starstruck young men and women were lured by the dazzle of Hollywood.

The war in Europe was expanding. The Allies needed aircraft and arms. Defense plants sprung up overnight in late 1939 and early 1940 with jobs for everyone.

When the United States was drawn into the war, production increased to produce ships, planes and tanks. With most of our able men off fighting, women became the backbone of the work force. More than 80 percent of our work force was female. What a great job they did.

When the war ended and the servicemen and women returned, homes had to be built to accommodate the population explosion in the West. Orange groves were cut down; corn and bean fields were plowed under for residential tracts; freeways went in everywhere. Los Angeles quickly became an asphalt jungle.

No, I don't like Los Angeles anymore—too many cars, too many apartments, too much smog, too many people and too many bumper-to-bumper freeways. But I have marvelous memories of L.A. when it was my kind of town.❖

Street Vendors of Chicago

By Roberta C. Gilbert

"Dad, Dad, hear the whistle? It's the waffle man. May we buy some?"

Dad usually answered "Yes" because he liked them, too. Mother sputtered, "Bob, why do you buy those things for the children? They taste like cardboard."

A few weeks later a different aroma filled the air as we heard the tinkling sound of the popcorn man. He came down Parkside Avenue pushing a bright red cart. On it was a glass box that held the popper, which was heated by a blue gas flame.

He filled a white paper bag with fluffy white kernels. Then he poured melted butter over it until the kernels were a golden yellow. With his big tin shaker, he dusted our treat with salt. No popcorn since has been as tasty—and it only cost a nickel.

Often on Mother's Day, a street singer with his accordion would come strolling down the street, singing and playing sentimental songs. One year it was a violinist; I believe everyone on the block gave him some money. He only came that one time; we hoped he got a full-time job.

It was a happy summer day when the organ grinder and his small monkey appeared. The monkey wore a scarlet embroidered vest with a matching cap. When we placed a few pennies in the tin cup he was holding, the monkey tipped his hat. The organ was shaped like a box, wound by hand and carried on a thick pole.

Another favorite was the balloon man who often arrived on Sunday afternoons with balloons in every color of the rainbow. My favorite was a bright, shiny, red one. If I wasn't careful, it might fly away. They cost 10 cents, and in those days that was expensive for a toy that might only be around for a few minutes, or at best, a couple of days. My Uncle Ed was a bachelor. If he was visiting us, he often bought balloons for my brother and me.

Saturday was special because that was the day we watched for the bakery truck. It was big and white, and smelled wonderful. There was an aisle down the middle with tempting treats on both sides—chocolate eclairs, cream rolls, hundreds of cookies and all kinds of breads. Mother didn't like baking in hot weather and she had a sweet tooth. Luckily for us, she often bought some goodies.

Other vendors came down the alleys. An important one was the iceman. We had a card about 8 inches by 12 inches. By the way it was turned, the iceman knew how much ice we needed. The driver attached his tongs to a big square of ice. He carried it into our house and put it in the icebox. Some men gave us chips of ice to suck. The boys would try to hitch a ride on the back.

The ragmen who drove dilapidated wagons and called out "Rags, bones and iron!" scared me a little. Perhaps it was because we never patronized them.

I can still recall my mother telling me to let her know if I heard the scissors grinder. We liked watching him at his dangerous work.

In the summers, fruit and vegetable men called their wares. We were delighted when we heard the call, "Fresh corn!" and hoped it was Golden Bantam.

I'd like to hear some of those calls again, especially "Popcorn!" But I think Mother was right about the waffles. ❖

Church at the Top of the Hill

By Betty C. Frazier

*I*t stands empty now, but for 90 years, St. Peter's Catholic Church stood small and proud, comfortable, warm and friendly, its doors open to the troubled, the tired, the sick, to any and all who needed consolation and close communication with their Master. It was a "Church at the Top of the Hill"—a tower of strength for the Catholic families of Wellsboro, a small town in north central Pennsylvania.

It was replaced by a magnificent new church in the 1970s—an edifice which has now been seasoned by countless masses, prayers and music of its own. The new church has just begun its story. It seems impossible to imagine that the new church will ever match the colorful history of the old, which flourished despite hardships and poverty and rigid church restrictions and traditions.

My early recollection of St. Peter's was of the hard, hard kneeling benches—which deeply impressed my bony knees.

But this is the story of "old" St. Peter's. In this fast-moving world, when man flies throughout the world in a matter of hours, when he has walked on God's moon and almost anything seems attainable except peace on Earth, it is special to be able to claim memories of five generations attending the same small church.

I am the oldest child in my family, and fortunately, I am able—if only vaguely—to recall my great-grandfather. Coming here from the "old country" across the Atlantic, he and his bride were among the first parishioners of St. Peter's, arriving even before the old church existed. Despite his death at a very old age in the 1930s, I can still see clearly his face with the map of Ireland etched upon it, the crop of white, bushy hair and his heavy mustache, and hear his brogue. Most of all, I remember his body, bent almost entirely in half from hard work and long years, and I can see his hands, which he always carried behind him, clasped upon his back.

In the early years, he had to walk a great distance to church, herding his family of eight children for what must have seemed endless miles, often through wet, muddy roads, drifts of snow and biting cold, as well as exhausting summer heat. It was the heat which finally claimed him, not on the way to church, but in his fields. His wife preceded him in

death by several years, and I have no memory of her, but his picture remains vivid in my mind's eye. The home where he raised his family and from which he left for Sunday mass still stands, and helps sustain my memory.

Half of his children left to make their way in other nearby communities. The rest remained—among them, the child who would become my grandmother. Through the years, it was no small chore for her and her family to get to St. Peter's for Sunday mass and holy days of obligation.

But they worked at their faith, and it seemed to be strengthened by their hardships. They all remained true to their beliefs, their church and their God until each was called by his Maker. Only after the passing of my grandmother in the early 1960s did I stop to think just what the word "grandmother" meant. I realized that the person who invented the word must have been blessed with such a one as mine.

One of my early memories is that of an altar boy leaping across one of the altar rails with his cassock ablaze after lighting the candles.

The next generation produced an even bigger brood, including my mother. Growing up as an only child after losing a young brother and sister, she relied on her nearby cousins for companionship. I have heard her tell of the kindly but strict priests who would be aghast at today's world.

My generation increased the family even more, but farther afield, adding only eight members to the congregation at St. Peter's. I lived in a household with grandparents, parents and two little sisters, and praying, reciting the rosary and attending mass came as naturally as breathing. My early recollection of St. Peter's was of the hard, hard kneeling benches—which deeply impressed my bony knees. I can recall almost uncontrollable spasms of childhood giggles and hiccups while in church. It brought us three little sisters immediate punishment— either stern glances from our elders, which hurt our pride, or a sharp elbow jab in the ribs from the senior members of the family, causing some physical pain as well.

Our catechism lessons were taught in the church after mass. Many family dinners were late while mothers taught.

We at St. Peter's were lucky to have an organ, but they were squeaky in those days, and singing in Latin didn't help matters musically. One of my early memories is that of an altar boy leaping across one of the altar rails with his cassock ablaze after igniting while he was lighting the candles.

The only new faces in the church during my earliest years seemed to be the priests; people didn't move about as much during the Depression and World War II. There came among us priests who were feared but respected; I can recall many favorites, as well. All tried to bring their people closer to God. And all, I'm sure, had numerous, whether they were "persons or purse strings."

Later came the weddings of family and friends; the baptisms and other sacraments of the Church—the conversions of the non-Catholic spouses, mine among them. These were joyful times spent with God in His house.

We recall the work "bees," especially the one held just before Easter when everything, including the statues of the saints, was scrubbed down by the Altar and Rosary Society.

Each generation had its share of grief—personal trials, disappointments, illnesses—which found them in church at any time of the week, day or hour, seeking strength and guidance to fight the battle of the moment. We remember the last goodbyes to our loved ones, when God's love was close and the walls of the little church embraced us tenderly. In the future, we would be reminded sharply of our loss many, many times, as we missed them kneeling beside us or seated in their favorite pew.

We recall seeing our only son serve as an altar boy—the first in our family to serve on that altar in 50 years. We recall this same child as a tiny tot just beginning to talk, greatly disturbed by the fact that the altar gate had not been tightly closed one day; in a loud "whisper" that echoed through the church, he said, "Mommy, someone forgot to close the gate on Jesus' playpen!"

We recall proudly and humbly entering the church for the first time with our baby daughter. In this church, we had prayed endlessly that God would bless our marriage with children. Our son, a long time coming and the first answer to our prayers, soon added his own

deeply serious prayers to ours for a little sister. Many candles burned themselves out as we prayed that God would find us to be a proper family, worthy to adopt a child. And prayers of Thanksgiving resounded within the church's stout walls when God did see fit to place these children into our hands, our hearts and home for loving care and guidance.

I remember running into church one Ash Wednesday, leaving a car pool of non-Catholic kindergarten children waiting while I got my ashes. When I returned to the car, one small boy who apparently felt left out exclaimed that he couldn't have any, "'cause my family doesn't have foreheads."

During those 90 years, parishioners made their earthly homes in many different houses. But the place where they worshipped remained the same. This house they shared with God was their strength, which many times made their other moves easier and less heartbreaking.

This, then, is one family's tribute to an old friend—a church no longer a church in the true sense of the meaning, but surely a friend.

Whether by desire or necessity, we have become a land of "nomadic people." Some enjoy this way of life; others have no choice. It is these, then, who will appreciate our feelings for old St. Peter's. People who have not known the feeling have missed a richness in their lives. By no means is their faith any less, and their devotion is no less; but they have never known the sense of truly belonging that we have.

Each family has had its own story. Some do not go back to the beginning, such as mine, and some may be more glowing or more painful. But all have involved life, death and the pursuit of happiness through their faith.

This, then, is one family's tribute to an old friend—a church no longer a church in the true sense of the meaning, but surely a friend. It will continue for many years in the memory of those who have loved it for so long as memory can serve us. We will take these memories with us to the new St. Peter's, but we will never really shut the door on "The Church at the Top of the Hill." ❖

Our Little Camp Town

By Audrey Burgess

The 1920s roared in like a big, bad bull, and fizzled out like a dying calf with the great Wall Street Crash of '29. Within 30 days of the stock market crash, the big coal mine, where my father worked, closed down, and we left our little camp town, which was way back in the Kentucky mountains, and moved to a small village in southern Ohio.

A camp town is generally owned by a big coal or lumber company. There were about 20 three- and four-room family houses, a few one-room shanty houses for bachelor miners, and a couple of big boarding houses in our camp town. We all rented from the coal company at reasonable prices.

Most of our houses came with a small garden plot, a good spring or well of water and an outside toilet. We all traded at the big general mercantile store owned by the company. If they didn't have what you wanted, they would order it for you, or we had mail order catalogs to order from. Our post office was inside the store.

Women canned, dried and pickled foods for winter. They sewed on pedal-type sewing machines and did lots of fancy needlework.

There was a small office building for the company doctor and a big ballpark where the men gathered on Sunday afternoons and holidays to play ball.

We walked one mile to the little country church or to the schoolhouse. These were not owned by the coal company. At church or school, we had pie suppers, picnic dinners, Labor Day bean dinners and Christmas programs. Now and then, a small traveling show put on a little play.

Folks gathered in each other's homes to have fish suppers and play their banjos, fiddles and guitars. There was lots of fishing and hunting in the nearby hills, and pitching horseshoes was another great pastime.

We bought our coal at a discount from the mine. It was delivered by horse and wagon. A stable and blacksmith shop operated on the back edges of our camp town, near the mine.

Women canned, dried and pickled foods for winter. They sewed on pedal-type sewing machines and did lots of fancy needlework. They were always busy making crepe-paper flowers and, occasionally, grave markers. The grave markers were glass fruit jars sealed with rubber bands and zinc lids so as to be weatherproof.

You wrote the name of the deceased and other vital statistics on a piece of paper, then held the paper to the inside of the jar, filling the jar with crepe-paper flowers to hold the paper in place. The flowers showed through the jar an inch or so on each end of the paper insert. You then dug a little nest about 1½ inches deep on the grave and laid the jar sideways in the nest, so you could read them. These markers held up very well. There were very few tombstones in these little mountainside cemeteries.

In wintertime, Mother would soak and cook dried apples, seasoning them with cinnamon and sugar. When cold, she would dip a cup of these apples out of the kitchen crock and stir them into a pan of clean snow. Then, using her hands, she made hard packed snowballs for us children as a treat. We loved to suck the sweet juice out and then eat the dried apple snowballs. They were delicious.

Often during the cold winter months, Mother would shell an ear of dried corn and parch dry a skilletful of the kernels to a golden brown, stirring them often. Then she lightly salted the still-hot, parched corn, and these crunchy-munchies, hot or cold, were truly a scrumptious treat.

In our camp town, the 1920s were filled with nice, old granny fortune tellers, midwives and women who had wardrobes of pretty, homemade aprons and who wore so-called bosom pins on their Sunday dresses. Men wore stickpins in their Sunday ties and were forever trading their pocketknives and watches with one another, trying to see who could get the most booty and best of the bargain.

In the fall, they made themselves pony kegs of white pear gin for their winter medicine.

Now and then, pack peddlers came through our camp town, selling small household notions, freshly caught fish or carts of fruit and vegetables. A knife sharpener came around in good weather to sharpen knives, scissors and tools.

There was always someone who went into the nearby woods and came back with stuff to

sell or trade—rabbits and squirrels in season, baskets of wild grapes, buckets of berries, sacks of nuts, bunches of herbs and roots or bittersweet for winter bouquets. Everybody worked or did these odd jobs to earn their dimes and quarters.

The 1920s were good years. There was no such thing as free welfare. It was 1930 when the tough years of the Great Depression set in, and the life of the rumbling '30s is yet another story. ❖

Front Porches

By Nancy Covert

Through the years they were the fair-weather center for the family. There are still front porches in the waterfront town where I live—porches furnished with wicker chairs, couches, tables and large planter boxes brimming with geraniums, petunias and nasturtiums—but few of them are shaded with old-fashioned striped canvas awnings. At least they've not succumbed to shading their decks with the trendy, U-shaped plastic awnings that have spread like a virus throughout many commercial districts.

An evening stroll around the neighborhood past these relics of a kinder, gentler era reminds me of the Northside Pittsburgh front porch—the setting for many childhood fantasies.

During my growing-up days in Pennsylvania, the arrival of the annual picnic season was heralded by the reappearance of the forest-green Adirondack furniture that had been stored under the porch since the previous fall.

The porch was our summer camp; it was also a backdrop for family portraits and a ringside seat during electrical storms.

Usually the weekend before Memorial Day, Dad unlatched the door to the crawl space beneath the porch and hauled out the stiff, green-and-orange striped canvas awnings and spider-egg-encrusted chairs and settee, freeing up the dirt-floored area that we annually claimed as our clubhouse.

During the summer the family regularly gathered for outdoor meals on the porch—not only on Memorial Day, the last day of school, Independence Day (we had a spectacular view of the city's fireworks displays from the porch) and Labor Day, but any warm day.

We grilled hot dogs, and enjoyed tender corn on the cob and Mom's fresh baked pies—and Grandma's German-style potato salad never tasted better.

Besides being the setting for family gatherings, the porch was our schoolhouse. Furnished with cast-off desks and supplies provided by my schoolteacher aunt, it became a place where I traveled through books to faraway places, to pioneer or medieval days.

On nights when we were allowed to sleep outside, the porch was our summer camp; it was also a backdrop for family portraits and a ringside seat during electrical storms, when the sky was split by mile-high lightning bolts and raw ozone filled the air.

When the snowy bridal wreath, mock orange and pale pink roses bloomed, my sisters and I dressed in cast-off gowns and held make-believe weddings on the steps of the "church."

In later years the porch served as an outdoor parlor where we four girls took turns sitting on the squeaky glider with our beaus. Mother, who chaperoned from a distance, was immediately alert when the glider stopped squeaking.

One summer, the porch was a hotel lobby when Mom devised a clever way to enlist our help with housecleaning. A "registration book" was placed on an entryway pedestal, while hand-lettered signs proclaimed that no liquor was served at this establishment. Our friends were "guests" who checked into the "hotel rooms" (that we'd thoroughly cleaned), and frosty glasses of lemonade washed down the freshly baked chocolate-chip cookies served in the hotel "dining room."

Old chenille bedspreads served as stage curtains that separated us "actors" from the audience who watched our front-porch variety shows. Porch railings served as practice bars, while curtained windows reflected slender dancers' silhouettes the summer the porch was a dance studio.

It was a "newspaper office" where we hand-lettered neighborhood gossip on blue-lined note paper and distributed copies door to door for a penny apiece.

The adults reclaimed the porch in the evenings, watching the world from its cushioned comfort. Sometimes after work, Dad sat on the middle step watering the lawn, the smoke from his Lucky Strike cigarette blending with the scent of freshly mown grass, while Mom mended clothes or tended the perennial flower garden that bordered the porch.

As we grew older, my parents talked about converting the porch into a downstairs bedroom, but it was only talk.

Nowadays, I have a small back porch furnished with wicker chairs and tables and shaded by vine maples. It's an ideal place to sit, reflect, plan—and watch my grandson play make-believe. ❖

The Old Front Porch

By Sue Lennon

Although it's many years ago,
It all comes back to me—
The Sunday afternoons at 4
When callers came to tea!

We'd sit upon the old front porch;
The swing would gently creak;
The children sat so prim and still,
For children must be meek!

The street would have a peaceful air,
As neighbors ambled by;
The grown-ups stopped their chatter then,
To wave a friendly "Hi!"

We'd sit out there till after dark,
As peaceful as could be,
Content with life about us,
With a friendly cup of tea!

Now years have changed so many things;
There's not much that we lack,
But somehow life's not quite the same
With porches in the back!

Views From a Swing

By Elizabeth R. Sphar

Remember the porch swing? That slatted swaying settee with bright flowered cretonne that hung from the porch ceiling by chains? That integral part of summer from which we could view comic and tragic happenings in our neighborhood?

I first felt its gentle rhythmic swaying as Mama lulled me to sleep while she rested in the cool of the evening after a busy day indoors. Creaking chains, chirping crickets and the steady whirrr of the hand mower Dad pushed across our lawn at dusk became my first and fondest lullabies.

Later, the swing became a castle, a cave, a fort and a tent when I was old enough to have a vivid imagination but too young to play tag or kick-the-can in the street.

I cherish memories of Mama moving the swing slowly back and forth, back and forth, as she read *A Child's Garden of Verses* or Hans Christian Andersen's *Fairy Tales* after I became too old for lullabies. Later, I curled up by myself to read *Elsie Dinsmore* and *The Five Little Peppers*, and still later, *The Circular Staircase* and *St. Elmo* on rainy days.

What gorgeous views of lightning storms I had from the shelter of our swing!

On bright nights after my folks had retired, my sweetheart and I could "spoon by the light of the moon." Fragrant rambler rose vines climbing the porch posts helped hide us from inquisitive eyes.

After my marriage, the porch swing was still the source of fond memories. It provided a place to sit and chat with the mailman, the iceman, the drayman, even peddlers. As we chatted, I shelled peas, snapped green beans, stemmed elderberries or pared apples. Such tasks were light when shared with a family member or a neighbor, when tongues worked as fast as fingers.

Our porch swing provided a grandstand seat for a continuing course in nature lore. From it I saw birds build their nests, sit on eggs, feed the newborn. I watched anxiously, chased predatory hawks and cats. I was both delighted and saddened when the nestlings were strong enough to fly away.

I watched flowers and shrubs bud, flower, fade. Daily I saw and heard a kaleidoscope of color and sound from the time we brought our porch swing from the storage shed and put it up in early May until we took it down in late October.

Our swing provided drama and humor, too. At least once or twice a summer, bolts and chains gave way and the swing fell down when seven or eight youngsters roughhoused on it—or when plump Aunt Ann and Uncle Ed plopped down onto it after a bounteous Sunday dinner.

Some said we never got anywhere while we swayed serenely back and forth. I claim we saw more of the world than those who now speed down freeways looking neither right nor left, or those who fly above the clouds and see nothing of our activities down below.

I knew when Mary and Bob, who lived down the street, were courting, knew when they quarreled, made up, married, had their first child, bought their first home.

I knew that old Mrs. Lapham's asthma was worse again when I saw Dr. Clark drive up to her home in his Model-T Ford.

I kept up with the latest styles when city cousins visited neighbors and promenaded to the bandstand or ice-cream parlor.

I saw youngsters graduate from foot scooters to bicycles to jalopies. I saw families progress from spring wagons to buggies, to surreys, to automobiles.

From our porch swing I saw the entire procession of life. And I still enjoy swinging back in time to relive those memorable days. ❖

Grandmother's Porch Swing

By Mary A. Morman

"There's no place to get away, to really hide," one of my children wailed in despair the other day.

I laughed, thinking of the size of our house and yard and the time required for cleaning and mowing all those square feet; then I sobered. He was right. Today's houses have no genuine hideaways, cubbyholes or sanctuaries like when I was a child. My place was just down the block—my grandmother's porch swing.

"Your grandchildren will sit in this swing," the carpenter told my grandmother in 1917 when he hung the porch swing for her. With a callused, tobacco-stained hand, he caressed the freshly painted slats, then thumped the back with his fleshy fist. "Yup, you can't beat this old swamp cypress. It takes to rough weather real good."

Everybody who tried the swing "took to it real good," according to my grandmother. The swing fostered neighborliness. Leisurely sitting there, you seemed to say, "I'm friendly; I'm approachable." Neighbors crossed the street; passersby stopped to chat; the mailman paused on his rounds; all were lulled by the to-and-fro movement and the cadence of creaking chains.

Swinging fast and high with the chains groaning and screaming was a dizzying, stomach-jolting adventure.

My father, my grandparents' eldest son, bought a house on the same street where his parents lived when he married. Disappointingly, that house had no porch to accommodate a porch swing for the children; however, we could run the half-block to Grandma's and use the swing if Grandma or Grandpa wasn't occupying it.

Sometimes Granny had friends for iced tea and they sat on the porch in lawn chairs while she sat in the swing—a queen on her throne, holding court. Her subjects were young mothers and middle-aged grandmothers. They dressed similarly in open-toed white pumps and printed cotton summer dresses with skirts so short (Dior was slow getting to Missouri) that we children, glimpsing the round rolled garters that held up their stockings, giggled in astonishment. Occasionally we were allowed to play nearby if we weren't too noisy. Sometimes we were very quiet, our ears perking when they spelled words they didn't want us to understand. More than once I showed too much interest and was chased away from the gossiping women.

On the main street in a small town, my grandparents' house was shaded by towering maples. The swing, further secluded by a honeysuckle-festooned porch railing, was a perfect place for remaining partially hidden while viewing a lot of what went on in town. After my grandfather retired, he spent a lot of time doing exactly that. He knew who rode by with whom, who walked out of town carrying a suitcase, and who didn't bother to brake for the stop sign on the corner.

When Grandpa napped afternoons in the back bedroom, the swing was ours. My brother, sister and I and assorted neighbor children and visiting cousins vied for the right to sit in the swing. It held three or four children, but sometimes we stacked in another layer.

In the swing I've eaten Grandpa's homemade ice cream, feasted on watermelon and had watermelon-seed-spitting contests, counted fireflies, swatted mosquitoes, savored violent thunderstorms, watched my dad and grandfather shoot off fireworks, dreamed my dreams, cried over teen-age traumas and contemplated real and imagined injustices.

In Grandma's swing, I rocked my baby sister and fought with my younger brother. I also sailed to Paris, flew to the moon, was captured by pirates, starred in a Hollywood film, conducted school, and played "Mother" in countless tea parties.

One summer the swing was off-limits. Hornets built a huge nest under the seat, and no one, not even my daring little brother, had the courage to defy such danger.

When we could swing, we really did—up to the ceiling, so high we could kick the mailbox next to the front door and just barely remain on the edge of the seat. Swinging fast and high with the chains groaning and screaming was a dizzying, stomach-jolting adventure. It was a matter of honor to not "chicken out." It was more acceptable to fall out trying to kick the mailbox than to not try at all.

The first great-grandchild to swing there is now a college sophomore. My own two children and four other great-grandchildren have played there. Undoubtedly, for them it has served as the Millennium Falcon or the space shuttle Columbia. Now and then I've seen a sad-faced child there, swinging slowly, scuffing his toes, sharing his burden with the listening swing, just as I once did. Recently I saw the youngest great-grandchild, hugging his teddy bear with one arm and a stuffed replica of E.T. with the other, gliding gently in the old porch swing. His dreamy expression told me he was far, far away. I longed to join him.

The swing has a fresh coat of misty gray paint and the cypress wood is still strong and solid. The house shows its age and the trees and shrubs aren't lush anymore. The wooden railing around the veranda is rickety and would not withstand the "King of the Mountain" abuse we gave it in the '40s and '50s, but the swing will entertain generations for years to come.

My grandmother hopes to rock her great-great-grandchildren in the swing. I believe she will. Recently, I told her that I had always longed for a porch swing of my own.

"If you had some way to take it back to Minnesota, you could have it," she said with a sly gleam in her keen black eyes. I suspect she knew exactly how much our vacationing family of four had crammed into our car.

I wouldn't have taken the swing had her offer been truly genuine—the swing is surely her vehicle for recalling and savoring scenes from the past—but for a minute I was tempted to accept her offer.

My suburban neighbors would probably think a porch swing tacky, but some days a comforting swing is just what my distraught teen-agers need—and so does their mother. ❖

Walking to School

By Dan B. McCarthy

*I*n the Bay View neighborhood on Milwaukee's southeast side, there's an elementary school that all eight children in our family attended and from which they eventually received diplomas.

School days for me began the year before 1929's Great Depression smothered the nation, and I received my diploma in 1936. No kids rode buses to our school. We walked, sometimes lingered or ran, depending on demands of the bank clock. Most kids didn't have watches.

School was a mile from our house. We had to cross two busy streets where electric streetcars ran and travel two tree-shaded side streets to reach the gray, stone, two-story building. Its wooden floors squeaked; the basement lunchroom smelled of orange peels. The adult friends we met along the way make up my strongest recollections of those school days.

When it comes to walking home from school, streets were safe then and we met a wonderful friend on each block.

Max, the neighborhood baker, was the first person we waved "good morning" to while passing the two large, plate-glass windows with "Max's Bakery" painted on each. Max's wave of flour-covered hands and his wide German smile started our new day's adventures. Max was kind and cheerful. When one of us ran to his bakery to buy a dozen hard rolls or schnecks, we knew there would be 13 in the sack when we got home. We learned about "the baker's dozen" from Max.

At the corner we all said, "G'mornin', Jim!" to the elderly policeman, recently transferred from walking the beat to guarding children at the busy Rosedale and Howell intersection. We used to run a half-block to that corner just to see who would be first for Jim to take in his big hands and swing up toward the sky. Then, stopping streetcar and auto traffic to walk us safely to the other curb, Jim would say, "You're all my kids!" He loved all the kids. We had great respect, friendship and love for Jim.

When warm spring days returned after the harsh winters blowing in off Lake Michigan, the icehouse on the vacant lot reopened and we'd again say, "Hi, Joe," to the man who was of husky build but soft of voice. Joe chipped 25-, 50- and sometimes 100-pound blocks from the larger ice chunks. Chips flew from his ice pick. He'd gather them into a little pile just inside the heavy wooden door, ready for us when we came along to and from school. We'd wrap our hankies around one end of an ice sliver and start up the hill, happy kids as ice numbed our tongues but cooled us. All Joe expected of us was "please" and "thank you," and he was a contented man, happy because he could give us "free ice" as we called it.

Each day, somewhere along Russell Avenue, we'd meet up with a short, thick-set man who, with wheelbarrow and push broom, kept streets tidy. From Jimmy it was always his cheery, "Hello, gang!" when we passed. On Fridays, he delighted in saying, "See you tomorrow!" knowing that we'd be back around home in overalls, not school clothes.

Our way to school brought us to a "Y" in the streets that left a large, paved, open area. City teamsters driving garbage wagons gathered at that collection place. They drew up with full wagons, set the brakes, unhitched the teams and led them to empty wagons. Occasionally, a huge Belgian horse got frisky and tried to bolt. That was big excitement, watching teamsters calm them. Most kids were amazed at how long the horses drank from the bathtub-size trough just next to the red fire hydrants.

When telephone company work crews had work along the street, they usually left their little two-wheel equipment trailers overnight up on the grass boulevard. They stopped work for the day just before afternoon classes ended and were gone when we passed. One kid discovered that there was usually a bucket of warm, melted wax under the canvas. If we located the bucket, we dipped our hands into the cooling wax, which stuck to our skin like grayish gloves. The rest of the way home, we waved waxy hands at our friends, trying to keep the "gloves" intact until suppertime.

Bill, who drove the bread truck, gave us day-old bread every day near the corner grocery. With his large basket of bread and cakes, Bill bounded out of the truck, took a couple of steps in our direction, greeted us, and handed us a loaf, sometimes two, and walked briskly away.

A half-century after our days of walking to school and 2,000 miles from "the old neighborhood," I was caught recently in traffic behind a huge, yellow school bus returning children to their corners. At every frequent stop, red lights flashed. The large STOP sign swung away from the bus' side. Motorists from each direction obeyed the signals. In the heavy traffic there was no way the bus could be passed. Stop. Start. Stop. Start.

I idled along behind and the thought occurred to me that, today, children come in contact with one adult outside school on traveling to classes: the driver. But where are the others we met in yesteryear? Where are Max, Jim, Joe, Bill, Jimmy and the teamsters whose names we seldom got to know?

Because we had adult friends at various points along our route to school a half-century ago, there was no cause for fear. Today, youths are cautioned that if strangers approach, they should run onto any front porch and ring the bell for help. Some communities have residents who place signs in their windows indicating that the home is a place of safety for school children who may be bothered by strangers.

Let the debates continue about the present and the Good Old Days. When it comes to walking home from school, give me the latter. Streets were safe then and we met a wonderful friend on each block. ❖

A Lion in the Streets

By Charles O'Dooley

Take a nice warm June morning, three kids and a huge dog named Mike. Mix them all together—and you have the makings of a very funny story.

It was the first day of summer vacation. School had let out the day before and my two sisters and I decided to celebrate our newfound freedom from books, long walks to school and paper-bag lunches by going swimming. Our dog, Mike, tagged along as always, wagging his tail and hanging his tongue out like he was smiling.

Let me tell you about Mike. We got him the year before at the county fair, where a little boy was selling puppies. He looked like a fuzzy teddy bear and we kids fell in love with him at first sight. After promising Mom we would feed and look after him, she relented and bought him from the boy for $2.

We had no idea he would grow into such a huge dog. He retained his fuzzy look, only the hair was much longer now. No one seemed to know just what breed Mike was. One man said he was an Irish wolfhound; others said he was just a mutt. Whatever he was, Mike was a big, friendly dog who enjoyed romping with children and was careful not to hurt them. When Pop had last weighed him in the barn, he topped the scales at 140 pounds.

Whatever he was, Mike was a big, friendly dog who enjoyed romping with children and was careful not to hurt them. When Pop had last weighed him in the barn, he topped the scales at 140 pounds.

The trouble began when we were passing Elder Simms' house. He was painting his front porch a dark green and was almost finished with the steps when his cat ran across the road in front of us. Now everyone knows what happens when a dog sees a cat. Mike was no exception. He took off after the cat, which took off running through the front yard to the rear of the house with Mike snapping at his heels.

What happened next you won't believe—but happen it did. The cat entered the kitchen door with Mike right behind him. The two ran through the house to the front door and the porch that Elder Simms had just finished painting. The cat leaped clear over the painted surface, but Mike didn't make it. He landed on the fresh paint with all four paws,

slipped and lost his balance. Mr. Simms and he rolled over and over in the green paint and ended up tumbling into the grass.

My sisters and I ran up to the porch as Mr. Simms was picking himself off the ground, brushing himself off and saying, "Well, I declare, I never saw anything like that in my life."

No need to tell you what Mike looked like. Instead of a big fuzzy bear, he looked more like the Jolly Green Giant. We apologized to Mr. Simms for Mike messing up his porch, but he was very nice about it and said you couldn't blame the dog—it was their nature to chase a cat when they saw one. We all stood there looking at Mike and his green coat and Mr. Simms started to laugh. He pointed at Mike and said he looked like a big green cucumber with legs, which made us laugh till our stomachs hurt. Poor old Mike was just sitting there with his head hung down, and if he could have talked I bet he would have said it wasn't funny to have green paint all over you.

Now the question was, how were we going to get the paint off Mike? Mr. Simms said it

was enamel and might be hard to remove. He got a big washtub from the barn and filled it with warm, soapy water. We kids held Mike in it while Mr. Simms tried to wash the paint off with a soft brush, but it was useless.

Since there was nothing more we could do, we decided to go on to the swimming hole and worry about Mike's new color later. But we never got there.

Mr. Moore's farm was at the top of the hill that led down to the creek where the swimming hole was. Mr. Moores raised sheep and this happened to be the day he was shearing them. His son, Lucas, was standing by the front-yard gate as we approached, and when he saw Mike, he asked what had happened. After explaining to him, he said there was only one solution— and that was to take him out to the shearing shed and have one of the men shear the hair off Mike. We thought that was a brilliant idea.

Mr. Moores was a jolly sort of man and not above pulling a joke on people. When he saw Mike, he began to laugh and said yes, he would help us. He grabbed Mike, who squirmed around so till we kids had to help hold him. As I said, Mr. Moores wasn't above a good joke, so he sheared the hair off Mike—all but a tuft at the end of his tail and the neck hair, which was left to form a mane. With Mike's size and the way he was sheared, he looked for all the world like a huge lion. In fact, Mr. Moores called him "Mike the Lion."

Mike didn't appreciate all of us gawking and laughing at him, so he took off running down the road back toward town, with us kids running right after him as fast as we could. But he was not to be caught and we didn't hear what happened until that evening when Pop sat us down and related all the trouble Mike had caused that day.

When Mike outran us, his first stop was the playground in the town park where a dozen or more children were playing on the swings and seesaws. An older boy who had gone hunting with his dad one time was the first to see Mike. He let out a yell, "Run! It's a mountain lion!" This threw the kids into a panic and some of them ran home, while others climbed the big oak tree in the middle of the playground.

Mike's next stop was the general store where he moseyed on in the front door and stood there looking around. Bob Billings, the storekeeper, was weighing up a sack of cornmeal for Old Lady Brown when he spied Mike standing in the door. He dropped the meal all over the floor and stood there with his mouth agape, unable to utter a word. Mrs. Brown turned to see what Bob was looking at and, upon seeing Mike, let out a scream and leaped clear over the counter into Bob, knocking him to the floor. (Bob said later he didn't know an 80-year-old woman could jump like that.)

"Run! It's a mountain lion!" This threw the kids into a panic and some of them ran home, while others climbed the big oak tree in the middle of the playground.

But the most remarkable thing that happened that day involved Mrs. Carter. Six years earlier, she had strained her back. The doctor advised her to use a wheelchair until her back healed. After a month, the doctor told her she didn't need the wheelchair anymore and could go back to walking again, but for some reason she didn't believe him. For six years, she stayed in her wheelchair, making her husband wait on her hand and foot. Then she saw Mike. Her husband, Charles, later related what had happened to the men at the general store, and they laughed until they cried. He and his wife were sitting in the back yard getting some sun, when Mike leaped over the back fence and came running toward them. When Mrs. Carter saw him, she screamed, leaped out of the wheelchair and ran like a rabbit to the kitchen door. The next day, Mr. Carter sold the wheelchair.

After all the trouble, Mike stayed in his doghouse for a week until he got his courage back. He wasn't the only one in the doghouse. My sisters and I were given a serious talking-to. We were about to lose our allowances for a month when Elder Simms came and told Mom and Pop what had happened and that it really wasn't our fault.

My sisters and I were sitting in the yard when he came out of the house after explaining to Mom and Pop. He smiled and said that when he first saw Mike after he was sheared, he thought he was a lion, too. With all the talk and good-natured laughing around town about Mike the Lion, Mom and Pop relented and didn't take our allowance. But after that, we kept Mike on a short leash and held on tight. ❖

Marian, the Librarian

By Betty Fay

When I was growing up back in the '30s and '40s, a kid was very much on his own in the find-something-to-do department. In winter we went sledding at Burke's Bottom; in summer we swam in the muddy waters of Lake Fork, and in between times, we went to the library.

I would have been lost without that little library. From the day of its founding until the time I went out on my own, I haunted it, prowling its shelves like a restless young ghost. It was my passport, you know, to places I never imagined I would see, my escape to the land of "Let's Pretend," my peep show affording occasional glimpses into the grown-up world I would one day be entertaining.

It was this latter category which eventually got me into trouble with Marian the librarian, and while I won the encounter, it was still like a little pleasure craft running broadside of the *Lusitania,* for Marian was a formidable foe! Stern of countenance and self-appointed guardian of young girls' morals, she ran a very tight ship. That library was as quiet as King Tut's tomb. Until you got used to her ways, you entered the sacred portals timidly, avoiding a direct confrontation with those gimlet eyes peering at you over the top of her spectacles like a hawk regarding a field mouse.

I was one of Marian's best customers, winning the prize each summer for most books read, and we had a great rapport. Until that fateful day in August, she was happy reminding me to spit out my bubble gum every time I walked through the door. On one occasion she advised me that shorts and halter tops were not only improper attire for a library, but unless I wanted the reputation for being a "fast one," I wouldn't be seen in them anywhere else either.

As I said, we learned to tolerate one another, and as long as I stuck to Nancy Drew, the Hardy Boys, and the thousand and one volumes of Zane Grey, Marian and I got on together. She'd stamp my weekly selection with approval oozing out of every pore, and I eventually earned the high honor of being able to check out an unlimited number of books at one time.

Such conviviality was not destined to endure, however, and one afternoon in the dog days of late August, I really came a-cropper with old Marian! There I was, scanning the shelves for a little tidbit to go along with my current diet of Grace Livingston Hill, when what did my Geiger counter eyes pick up but a meaty-looking volume titled *Murder at Leisure.* Plucking it from its place on the shelf, I plunked it down on the desk in front of Marian. She recoiled like it was a basketful of cobras.

"You don't want this," she hissed. When I hissed right back that I really did, it was like throwing down a gauntlet. She said, "Not without a note from home you don't."

I trudged home furiously over the hot brick sidewalks, collected a note from one of those two maiden lady sisters who, with the help of God, were frantically trying to see me through the turbulence of pre-adolescence, and marched myself back to confront Marian.

She dutifully checked the book out to me then, after reading the note in frosty silence. Bristling with disapproval, she stamped the card and handed me the book without another word, even though her expression clearly implied that my whole family and I were going to the hot place on a greased toboggan!

All of that was very long ago. I read the controversial book and many others like it and Marian gradually got over her huff. When I think of her now, I do so fondly because I remember she was associated with the only institution in town that was absolutely free, and in those days, free was one of the beautiful words. ❖

The Old Neighborhood

By Norma S. Archer

*W*e grew up on Hale Avenue in White Plains, N.Y. It was a quiet, rural neighborhood with big open fields and meadows of wildflowers to roam in—and an ideal spot to raise children.

We lived for many years in one of the four houses at the beginning of the street, with the same three families as neighbors. We were the Scholls; next-door were the Eschenfelders (commonly referred to as "Esch" at their request), the Waterhouse family and the Ackermans. In time, we all became very close.

On many hot summer evenings, long before television was even thought of, my mother, my dad and my sister, Gloria, sat on the front porch in rockers or the big wicker chair with the round back. I ensconced myself on the steps to knit. Before you knew it, a neighbor would drop by and join us. Out would come the ice-cold lemonade, cookies or whatever else happened to be available. There would be pleasant conversation as we quietly relaxed and watched the daylight turn to dusk, then darkness, bringing the comfortable, cool night air.

There would be pleasant conversation as we watched the daylight turn to dusk, then darkness, bringing the comfortable, cool night air.

During the day, my sister and her little friend Bea often sat on the porch, rocking in their chairs and calling, "How-do," to passersby. People usually answered them, but one day someone made no response. The children stared at each other aghast, then sniffed, and with great annoyance exclaimed, "Stuck-ups!"

Most of the time, Bea and Gloria got along quite well, but like most children, they had occasional spats. One doozie was so bad that they wouldn't speak to each other.

Worse still, our moms got involved and they didn't speak to each other—for days—until they realized that the kids had forgotten about the fight long ago, and were playing together as usual! Our moms then decided not to get involved in the kids' fights again, and they never did.

At the top of the hill was the armory, where the American flag flew from a pole. Whenever we were going out, we would ask our grandmother, who lived with us, to predict the weather. Grandma would walk to the front porch, look up at the flag to see how the wind was blowing, and give us her weather report. "You'd better take an umbrella," she would advise sometimes—or, "It will be fine." Most of the time, she was right!

Once there was a demonstration at the armory during which a man was put into a wooden box and buried in the armory's front yard for some hours. It was said he swallowed his tongue and went into "a cataleptic state." I had an awful sinking feeling that I'd never see him alive again as they shoveled dirt on top of the box. Hours later, when they dug him up and I saw that he was still alive, I certainly felt relieved.

Another diversion the armory provided was a cooking school. Since cooking was very popular with us, Millie Ackerman, Mom, Gloria and I attended. We paid close attention as the instructor made all sorts of goodies—great dinner dishes, fancy pies and cakes—and gave them away to members of the audience when they were finished.

In addition, a number of bags of groceries were raffled off at the end of each session. As the time for the giveaways approached, a ripple of excitement ran through the crowd. We wondered if we would be lucky enough to win. And win we did! Mom and I both happily collected bags of groceries. But when Millie's number was called, she became so flustered that she lost her balance and slipped. Her folding chair collapsed, and down she went onto the floor, her legs waving in the air! At first we were concerned that she might be hurt, but she got up and laughed as she went to collect her prize. Relieved, we all joined in the laughter, too.

During these happy years, our beloved next-door neighbor, Mr. "Esch," planted

and tended a beautiful garden with many varieties of colorful flowers. We were all very proud of it and were sad to see it go. After a while, the city took over the lot and made it into a quoits field. Many of us enjoyed playing there, and you could hear the clinking of the heavy horseshoes as we got our exercise.

Mrs. Eschenfelder, "Eschie," as we called her, was a stout, friendly, good-natured woman. It was easy to see that she liked children, for she never refused my occasional question, "Mrs. Esch, would you please play 'hang the man' with me?" I now realize it must sometimes have been very inconvenient for her. She would take me into her house, have me sit down, and draw lines to make the place to "hang the man." Then I would guess what

letters filled the spaces she made for the words she chose. Often she gave me some of her delicious sugar or spice cookies, too.

A member of the Hale Avenue animal population was the Eschenfelders' beautiful collie, Lassie, with a long, prettily pointed nose. She had a gentle disposition and we all loved her. It seemed natural for me to offer this friend a lick of my ice-cream cone. However, Lassie didn't understand my offer and gobbled the whole ball of ice cream, much to my dismay!

Once an old buggy appeared around the corner near Pauling Street, where some of our friends lived. I don't know how it got there, but we took advantage of the situation and had a lot of fun with it. Two of the neighborhood boys were the "horses" and pulled a bunch of us girls around in it.

Other neighborhood activities took place at Bloomingdale Pond, several blocks away. It was situated on a large tract of land and a high iron fence surrounded it, as mentally ill patients were hospitalized there. We were warned to be very careful when we went, but we never had problems. We entered at the spot where two bars in the fence were pushed apart. Every spring, kids carrying long-handled nets and pails would pass our house on the way to the pond to catch goldfish. We would join in the fun. We waded and caught salamanders and tadpoles in the meandering brook that emptied into the pond.

In winter, the pond was a great place to skate. One day my sister and I found that we were the only skaters. Nevertheless, we donned our skates and started across the pond. Suddenly, with every stroke of our skates, we heard the ice cracking loudly under our feet as we neared the large noisy waterfall that emptied into a second brook. We were skating on dangerously thin ice! We veered quickly and skated as fast as we could toward shore and jumped off the ice—just in time to see it break apart where we had been skating a moment before!

Many years have passed since we all moved away from Hale Avenue, but we still keep in touch. I'm sure none of us will ever forget the old neighborhood where we had so much fun and excitement. We always knew we were welcome to stop and chat awhile with folks who seemed more like family than friends and neighbors. ❖

My Old Neighborhood

By Mildred Summers

I miss my old neighborhood; I drove back there today.
Somebody tore our house down, And took the swing away.

My heart sank when I saw it; I always loved it so;
They cut down the trees I planted, So many years ago.

I went over to my friend's house, And had a cup of tea;
Oh, I miss my old neighborhood, And I hope it misses me.